TART

TART

Sweet & savoury recipes

hamlyn

Notes

Ovens should be preheated to the specified temperature. If using a fan-assisted oven, follow the manufacturer's instructions for adjusting the time and temperature. Grills should also be preheated.

This books includes dishes made with nuts and nut derivatives. It is advisable for those with known allergic reactions to nuts and nut derivatives and those who may be potentially vulnerable to these allergies, such as pregnant and nursing mothers, invalids, the elderly, babies and children, to avoid dishes made with nuts and nut oils. It is also prudent to check the labels of preprepared ingredients for the possible inclusion of nut derivatives.

The Department of Health advises that eggs should not be consumed raw. This book contains some dishes made with raw or lightly cooked eggs. It is prudent for more vulnerable people such as pregnant and nursing mothers, invalids, the elderly, babies and young children to avoid uncooked or lightly cooked dishes made with eggs.

Fresh herbs should be used unless otherwise stated. If unavailable use dried herbs as an alternative but halve the quantities stated.

Meat and poultry should be cooked thoroughly. To test if poultry is cooked, pierce the flesh through the thickest part with a skewer or fork – the juices should run clear, never pink or red.

First published in Great Britain in 2004 by
Hamlyn, a division of Octopus Publishing Group Ltd
2–4 Heron Quays, London E14 4JP

ISBN 0 600 61033 0
EAN 9780600610335

A CIP catalogue record for this book is available from
the British Library

Printed and bound in China

10 9 8 7 6 5 4 3 2 1

Contents

Equipment

Most cooks would agree that the secret of good pastry lies not in expensive gadgets but in having a cool, quick hand. However, there are a few items of equipment that are essential for making good pastry.

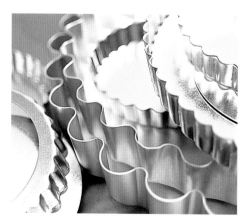

Scales Getting the correct proportions of flour and fat (and sugar, when you are making sweet pastry recipes) is actually more important than the precise quantities of each ingredient. It is sometimes possible to weigh the ingredients straight into the mixing bowl, or you may prefer to measure and add each ingredient separately.

Working surface Pastry should be rolled out on a clean, cool, level surface that has been lightly dusted with flour. It's possible to buy special boards or you may prefer to use a work top.

Mixing bowls Always use a bowl that is large enough to hold comfortably all the ingredients you will be using. Having to transfer to a larger bowl halfway through a recipe because clouds of flour are covering your work top can be both tricky and messy.

Measuring spoons Ingredients are often given in teaspoons or tablespoons. All spoon measures in the recipes in this book are assumed to be level (1 teaspoon equals 5 ml and 1 tablespoon equals 15 ml). It is worth buying a set of measuring spoons so that you can accurately add ¼ or ½ teaspoon quantities as necessary, as well as larger quantities of both liquid and dry ingredients.

Sieve Sift the measured flour or flours (and salt, if required) into the mixing bowl. This will remove any lumps and separate the grains so that the fat is more easily coated and assimilated into the dough.

You will also need a sieve for dusting finished sweet tarts with icing sugar or cocoa powder. Hold the sieve to one side of the tart, then shake or tap it lightly as you move it across the surface to achieve a light, even covering. If you wish, you can lay a doily or stencil over the surface before you begin, to create a pattern in icing sugar.

Food processor A food processor can be used to make successful pastry quickly. It reduces the time you have to handle the dough, which can be helpful in hot weather or if you have warm hands. Take

care not to overmix the fat with the flour, however. A few short bursts will allow you to judge the breadcrumb stage. You may find you need a little more water than if you are mixing by hand, but this is largely a matter of the type of flour you are using and the fat you have chosen, so add any water little by little rather than all at once.

Pastry brushes You will need a fairly broad brush for applying melted butter to sheets of filo pastry, for example, and a finer brush for more detailed work, such as applying glazes to small pastry decorations.

Clingfilm When you make pastry the gluten in the flour becomes elastic. It is important that the pastry is allowed to rest so that it does not shrink and become distorted when it is cooked. When you chill unrolled pastry, cover it closely with clingfilm or put it inside a plastic bag. If the surface of the pastry comes into contact with the air it will form a skin, which will crack when it is rolled out. When you have rolled out and lined the tart tin or tins, do not trim off the excess pastry until you have allowed the pastry to rest again.

Baking sheets You can either lightly grease a baking sheet or use a sheet of greaseproof baking paper. When placing a tart on a baking sheet, it is a good idea to put the baking sheet in the oven while it is preheating to warm it. The base of the pastry will then cook more quickly and will be crisper.

Tins and dishes Tart tins with loose bases make removing pastry cases from the tin easy, but lined and greased tins and dishes with straight and fluted sides can also be used. Small pastry cases for tartlets can be cooked in small cake or muffin tins. Metal

containers usually give better results than ceramic ones because they conduct heat more efficiently.

Cutters Small tarts can easily be cut out with a pastry cutter, and you will find a wide range of plastic and metal cutters in all kinds of shapes and sizes in any cook shop. Running the point of a sharp knife around upturned saucers and bowls of various sizes is a quick and convenient way of cutting out larger pastry circles.

Baking beans Many pastry cases are baked blind – that is, they are wholly or partly cooked before the filling is added so that the liquid in the filling does not soak into the pastry and make it soggy. To prevent the pastry from rising during the initial cooking, a circle of greaseproof paper can be put inside the pastry case and held in place by baking beans. Dried beans or lentils can be used instead although they do not have as long a life as ceramic beans.

Making pastry
Pastry-making is not an esoteric art, but a matter of following a set of simple rules, the most important of which is to keep everything cool – hands, head, equipment and ingredients.

Choice of flour

Plain white flour is the best choice for most recipes, giving a light, crisp pastry. Self-raising flour gives a softer, sponge-like texture and should be used for suet crust, which will be heavy without a raising agent. Wholemeal flour, or a mixture of half wholemeal and half white, can be used for shortcrust pastry, but it tends to give a heavy, crumbly dough, which can be difficult to handle. Puff, flaky or rough puff pastries are usually made with strong plain flour, because its high levels of gluten give the dough more elasticity and strength.

Choice of fat

The type of fat you use will affect the texture as well as the flavour of the pastry. It should be cold, so only remove it from the refrigerator shortly before use to make it easier to handle.

Butter, preferably unsalted, gives the best colour and flavour, but when it is used on its own it can be rich and oily. Margarine is good for colour but has an inferior flavour to butter; results will depend on the quality. Soft margarine should be used for fork-mix, all-in-one pastry only. Lard, or a good quality vegetable fat, gives a good short, crumbly texture, but it lacks flavour

and colour when used on its own.

The best shortcrust pastry is made using equal quantities of butter or margarine with lard or white vegetable fat.

Secrets of successful pastry

- Measure the right proportions of fat to flour, according to the type of pastry. For shortcrust pastry, use double the weight of flour to fat. Richer short pastries use a higher proportion of fat to flour.

- Unless you are making choux pastry, keep everything, including your hands, as cool as possible.

- When you are rubbing in fats use only the very tips of your fingers to keep the mixture cool. Lift the fingers high and let the crumbs run through them back into the bowl. If you use a food processor pulse the power to make sure that the pastry is not overmixed.

- When you are rolling out and shaping pastry don't handle it more than necessary as this will make it heavy.

- Don't add the liquid all at once. Flours vary in absorbency, and too much liquid can make the pastry heavy.

How much pastry?

When a recipe gives a guide to the quantity of shortcrust pastry required, the weight refers to the amount of flour. For example, if the recipe requires 200 g (7 oz) shortcrust pastry or rich shortcrust pasry, make the dough from 200 g (7 oz) flour, plus fat and other ingredients in proportion. Here is a rough guide to how much pastry you will need for different sizes of tart tin:

TART TIN DIAMETER	PASTRY QUANTITY
18 cm (7 inch)	125 g (4 oz)
20 cm (8 inch)	175 g (6 oz)
23 cm (9 inch)	200 g (7 oz)
25 cm (10 inch)	250 g (8 oz)

Water

Use as little water as possible to bind the dough. Adding too much water can make the dough sticky and difficult to handle and the cooked pastry tough. Always try to use cold water; in warm weather iced water is ideal. For normal shortcrust pastry you will need about 1 teaspoon of water for each 25 g (1 oz) of flour. Although the amount will vary a little depending on the absorbency of the flour, this is a useful guideline to follow. If you are adding egg or egg yolk use proportionately less water.

Sugar

Some rich pastries, including pâte sucrée, use a small amount of sugar to give a crisp texture and golden colour.

Eggs

Egg, usually only the yolk, is used to bind rich pastries. It also adds colour to pastry. Beat it lightly with a fork before adding it to the other ingredients.

Chilling and resting

With the exceptions of choux pastry and suet crust, pastry benefits from resting for about 30 minutes before baking. This reduces shrinkage during cooking and is particularly important for pastries that are handled a great deal during preparation, such as puff or rough puff. Wrap the pastry in clingfilm to prevent it from drying out and put it in the refrigerator.

Cooking

When you are making pastry, it is vital to preheat the oven thoroughly first, particularly for pastries with a high fat content, which should be cooked at a high temperature for light, crisp results.

Using pastry
Don't handle pastry more than necessary and always roll it away from you, using light, even pressure and adding as little extra flour as possible, as too much can result in tough pastry.

Rolling out

Dust a cool work surface and your rolling pin lightly with flour. Roll lightly and evenly in one direction, always away from you, moving the pastry around by a quarter turn occasionally. Try to keep the pastry even in shape and thickness. Avoid stretching the pastry, which will cause it to shrink during cooking. Depending on the recipe, shortcrust pastry is usually rolled to about 3 mm (⅛ inch) thick; puff pastry can be rolled slightly thicker, to about 5 mm (¼ inch).

Lining a tart tin

Put the flan ring or tart tin on a baking sheet. Roll out the pastry to about 5 cm (2 inches) larger all around than the diameter of the ring or tin. Roll the pastry loosely around the rolling pin, lift

it over the tin, then carefully unroll it into the tin.

Gently ease the pastry into the tin, pressing it into the flutes with your finger and taking care not to stretch it or leave air gaps underneath. Turn any surplus pastry outwards from the rim, then roll the rolling pin straight over the top so that the surplus pastry is cut and falls away, to leave a neat edge.

Baking blind

This is the process of part-baking pastry in the tin before the filling is added, to ensure crisp results. The pastry is weighted down to prevent it from bubbling up or falling down around the sides.

Line the tart tin with the rolled-out dough as usual and prick the base of the pastry with a fork, so that any air trapped

underneath can escape rather than cause the pastry to bubble up.

Place a square of nonstick baking paper in the pastry case and, taking care not to damage the edges of the pastry, half-fill the paper with dried beans or ceramic baking beans. Bake as instructed in the recipe, usually for 10–15 minutes, then remove the paper and beans. Return the pastry case to the oven for about 5 minutes to crisp the base if necessary. Crumpled foil can be used instead of beans.

Using filo pastry

Filo pastry has a reputation for being difficult to handle, but if you follow these simple guidelines, you will find that it is no more difficult to use than any other pastry. To keep filo soft and workable, make sure that the pastry is covered all the time you are not actually working on it. Lay a sheet of clingfilm or a damp cloth over it or keep it wrapped, because it will become brittle and break easily if it dries out.

Work quickly, using up any broken or torn pieces of filo pastry between whole sheets – no one will notice. Do not moisten filo pastry with water, which makes the sheets stick together and disintegrate; keep the work surface dry for the same reason. Use fat, such as melted butter, to seal edges and to brush the pastry for crisp results.

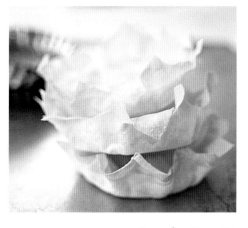

Pastry decorations

A modest decoration is part of the traditional look of pies and tarts. Leaves, a lattice and fancy edges all enhance the appeal and are very simple to make.

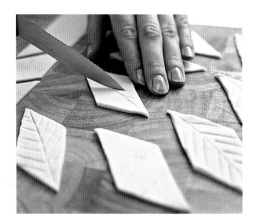

Pastry leaves

A decorative border of pastry leaves around the rim of a tart works particularly well on a tart with a smooth plain filling such as the *Pumpkin pie (see page* 93). Holly leaves make an attractive addition to Christmas tarts. Pile any pastry trimmings on top of each other in a stack – do not press them into a ball, because they will rise unevenly. Roll the pastry out to about 3 mm (⅛ inch) thick.

Cut the pastry into long, narrow strips, about 2.5 cm (1 inch) wide. Make diagonal cuts across the strips to create diamond shapes. Press a knife gently against the pastry, taking care not to cut right through, to mark the veins on each leaf.

Arrange the leaves so that they overlap on top of the pie, securing them to the crust by brushing them underneath with a little water, milk or beaten egg.

Making a pastry lattice

A lattice of pastry looks attractive on both savoury and sweet tarts and pies. Keep the lattice strips apart, leaving wide gaps to show the filling or arrange them almost touching to make a closed lattice top.

Cut the pastry into long, narrow strips. Starting at one side of the tart, overlap the strips, weaving them alternately under and over each other, to make a wide trellis. Attach the strips to the edge of the tart by moistening each one with a little water and pressing it lightly in place. Trim off the excess with a knife.

Making decorative edges

Plait Cut three long, narrow strips of pastry. Pinch them together at one end and press this on the rim of the pie. Plait the

against the top of the pastry rim and press the blade of a knife horizontally into the cut pastry edge, making a series of shallow cuts. Do this all around the edge.

Scallops This decorative finish to a pie crust adds a professional touch to a pie or tart and helps to firmly seal the edge of the tart. Place the knife blade at a vertical angle against the pastry edge and press your fingertip next to it on the rim. Make a vertical cut, pulling slightly upwards, to create a scallop. Continue around the edge at intervals of about 1.5 cm (¾ inch) all around the tart.

strips around the pie, joining in extra lengths of pastry as necessary to go all around. Tuck the ends under.

Twist Cut two long, thin strips of pastry and pinch them together at one end. Attach this to the pie rim and then twist the strips gently, arranging them around the pie edge as you go.

Flaking or knocking up It's important to seal the pastry neatly to prevent fillings from leaking out. Hold one finger lightly

Crimping This is a quick and simple alternative to flaking and scalloping pastry edges. Push the finger of one hand into the top of the pastry rim. At the same time, pinch the outer edge with the finger and thumb of the other hand, pinching the pastry to a point. Continue crimping all around the edge of the pie.

Shortcrust pastry
The classic choice for savoury and sweet everyday dishes, shortcrust pastry is easy to handle and holds its shape well for pies and tart cases.

PREPARATION TIME: about 10 minutes, plus chilling
MAKES 200 g (7 oz)

200 g (7 oz) plain flour
pinch of salt
100 g (3½ oz) fat, such as equal quantities of butter and white vegetable fat
2–3 tablespoons iced water

1 Sift the flour and salt into a bowl. Cut the fat into small pieces and add it to the flour.

2 Use your fingertips to rub the fat into the flour very lightly and evenly until it begins to resemble fine breadcrumbs.

3 Sprinkle the water over the surface and stir with a palette knife until the mixture begins to clump together.

4 Turn out the pastry on to a lightly floured surface and press it together lightly with the fingers. Chill for about 30 minutes before use.

Rich shortcrust pastry
The inclusion of an egg yolk gives a fine, crispy pastry that is ideal for sweet tarts but can also be used for savoury tarts if you need a standing crust.

PREPARATION TIME: about 10 minutes, plus chilling

MAKES 200 g (7 oz)

200 g (7 oz) plain flour

pinch of salt

100 g (3½ oz) fat, such as equal quantities of butter and white vegetable fat

1 egg yolk

2–3 tablespoons iced water

1 Sift the flour and salt into a bowl. Cut the fat into small pieces and add it to the flour.

2 Use your fingertips to rub the fat into the flour very lightly and evenly until it begins to resemble fine breadcrumbs.

3 Add the egg yolk and stir with a palette knife until the mixture begins to clump together. Add just enough cold water if necessary to make a firm dough.

4 Turn out the pastry on to a lightly floured surface and press it together lightly with the fingers. Chill for about 30 minutes before use.

Pâte sucrée
A sweet, enriched shortcrust pastry, this has a rich, biscuit-like texture suitable for sweet tarts and pastries. This makes enough pastry to line a 20 cm (8 inch) tart tin.

PREPARATION TIME: about 10 minutes, plus chilling
MAKES 175 g (6 oz)

175 g (6 oz) plain flour
pinch of salt
75 g (3 oz) unsalted butter, slightly softened
2 egg yolks
1 tablespoon cold water
40 g (1½ oz) caster sugar

1 Sift the flour and salt into a pile on a cold work surface and make a well in the centre.

2 Add the butter, egg yolks, water and sugar to the well and use the fingertips of one hand to work them together into a rough paste. The mixture should resemble scrambled egg.

3 Gradually work in the flour with your fingertips to bind the mixture into a smooth dough. Press together lightly and form into a ball. Wrap in clingfilm and chill for about 30 minutes before use.

Puff pastry

Well-made puff pastry will rise to about six times its height when it is cooked. Although it has a reputation for being difficult to make, the most important guideline is to keep all the ingredients cool.

PREPARATION TIME: about 30 minutes, plus chilling
MAKES 250 g (8 oz)

250 g (8 oz) plain flour
pinch of salt
250 g (8 oz) cooled butter in one piece
1 teaspoon lemon juice
150 ml (¼ pint) iced water

1 Sift the flour and salt into a bowl. Use your fingertips to rub in a quarter of the butter until it resembles breadcrumbs. Add the lemon juice and most of the water. Mix to a dough and gradually add the rest of the water to form a dry dough.

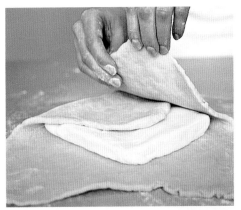

2 On a floured work surface knead the dough into a ball and flatten. Wrap it in clingfilm and chill for about 30 minutes.

3 Put the rest of the butter between two sheets of clingfilm and roll out to a square about 1 cm (½ inch) thick. Unwrap the chilled pastry and roll it out to form a square large enough to wrap round the butter. Put the butter in the centre of the pastry square and fold over the edges to encase the butter completely.

4 Dust the work surface and rolling pin and roll out the pastry to a long rectangle about 1 cm (½ inch) thick. Fold the bottom third on to the middle third, then fold the top third over the top. Rewrap and chill for 15 minutes.

5 Return the pastry to the work surface with a short edge facing towards you. Press down on the edges slightly then roll it out into a rectangle and fold as before. Repeat this six times, then chill the pastry. Roll it out to its final shape, then chill again for 30 minutes. 'Knock up' the edges so that the layers rise properly.

Cheat's rough puff pastry

This deliciously rich and crisp, slightly flaky pastry is ideal for single-crust pies, pasties or sweet pastries. It does not rise as much as puff pastry, but it is far simpler to make.

PREPARATION TIME: about 10 minutes, plus chilling
MAKES 250 g (8 oz)

250 g (8 oz) plain flour

pinch of salt

175 g (6 oz) butter, thoroughly chilled, until almost frozen

about 150 ml (¼ pint) iced water mixed with 2 teaspoons lemon juice

1 Sift the flour and salt into a bowl. Holding the butter with cool fingertips or by its folded-back wrapper, grate it coarsely into the flour. Work quickly before the butter softens from the heat of your hand.

2 Stir the grated butter into the flour with a palette knife, then sprinkle with just enough iced water to start binding the ingredients into a dough. Press the dough lightly together with your fingertips.

3 Turn out the dough on to a lightly floured surface and roll it out into an oblong about three times longer than it is wide.

4 Fold the bottom third of the pastry up and the top third down, then press around the sides with a rolling pin to seal the layers together lightly. Chill for about 30 minutes before use.

Choux pastry

This breaks all the rules for pastry making: it needs lots of heat and firm handling for good results. Use it for sweet or savoury buns, profiteroles, beignets and éclairs.

PREPARATION TIME: about 10 minutes
MAKES 75 g (3 oz)

75 g (3 oz) plain flour

pinch of salt

50 g (2 oz) unsalted butter

150 ml (¼ pint) water or equal quantities of water and milk

2 large eggs, lightly beaten

1 Sift the flour and salt on to a sheet of greaseproof paper.

2 Place the butter and water in a saucepan and heat gently until the butter melts, then bring to the boil. Do not bring to the boil before the butter melts.

3 Draw the pan off the heat and immediately add the flour, all at once. Beat with a wooden spoon or electric hand mixer just until the mixture forms a smooth ball which leaves the sides of the pan clean. Do not overbeat at this stage or the paste will become oily.

4 Cool the mixture for 2 minutes. Gradually add the eggs, beating hard after each addition, and continue to beat until the mixture is smooth and glossy. The paste should be just soft enough to fall gently from the spoon. Use the pastry immediately or cover closely and chill until needed.

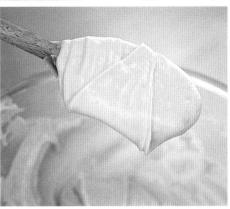

Savoury *The fillings for savoury tarts range from the simple cream, eggs and bacon of a classic Quiche Lorraine to the spicy, oriental-style of Crispy Duck Tarts. Whether you want a quick, informal lunch or a dish to impress dinner-party guests, there is a tart for every occasion.*

Experiment with different combinations of fillings to ring the changes on old favourites. If you are worried about the calories in fillings that include cream, use crème fraîche or low-fat soft cheese instead. Mascarpone cheese, which can be found in the chiller cabinets of all supermarkets and many smaller food stores, gives fillings a wonderfully smooth, creamy texture, but you can use cream cheese with equally good results.

Goats' cheese & cherry tomato puff

Serve this delicious tart hot either as a starter or for a light lunch with a salad of bitter leaves. If possible, use a mixture of red and yellow tomatoes.

PREPARATION TIME: 15 minutes

COOKING TIME: 20–25 minutes

OVEN TEMPERATURE: 220°C (425°F), Gas Mark 7

SERVES 4–6

250 g (8 oz) puff pastry, defrosted if frozen

2–3 tablespoons olive oil

250 g (8 oz) cherry tomatoes, sliced

250 g (8 oz) firm goats' cheese, sliced

2 teaspoons chopped thyme

salt and pepper

1 Make the pastry (*see pages* 17–18). Roll it out and trim to a 23 cm (9 inch) round. Transfer to a prepared baking sheet and brush lightly with olive oil.

2 Spread half the sliced cherry tomatoes over the pastry to within 2.5 cm (1 inch) of the edge.

3 Arrange the goats' cheese over the top and scatter with the remaining cherry tomatoes. Season with a little salt and pepper. Sprinkle with the thyme and drizzle 1–2 tablespoons of olive oil over the top.

4 Bake in a preheated oven for 20–25 minutes until the pastry is risen, crisp and golden-brown.

Aubergine, tomato & haloumi tart

Haloumi is a creamy-textured, slightly sharp Greek cheese that goes particularly well with aubergine. If you can't find haloumi use mozzarella instead.

PREPARATION TIME: 20 minutes

COOKING TIME: 35 minutes

OVEN TEMPERATURE: 200°C (400°F), Gas Mark 6

SERVES 4

250 g (8 oz) puff pastry, defrosted if frozen

beaten egg or milk, to glaze

1 tablespoon sun-dried tomato paste

375 g (12 oz) aubergines, sliced

2 tablespoons olive oil

5 ripe tomatoes, sliced

125 g (4 oz) haloumi cheese, thinly sliced

2 teaspoons chopped oregano

50 g (2 oz) green olives, pitted and halved

salt and pepper

1 Make the pastry (*see pages* 17–18). Roll it out to a 25 cm (10 inch) square and put it on a prepared baking sheet. Use a sharp knife to make two L-shaped cuts in the pastry 2.5 cm (1 inch) in from the edges, leaving the two opposite corners uncut (*see picture on page* 58). Brush the edges of the pastry with water.

2 Lift up one cut corner and draw it across the pastry to the opposite cut side. Repeat with the other cut side to form a case. Brush the edges of the pastry with egg or milk and prick the base. Spread the tomato paste over the base of the pastry case.

3 Brush the aubergine slices with oil and cook under a preheated moderate grill until lightly browned. Turn, brush again with oil and brown on the other side.

4 Arrange the aubergine slices, tomatoes and cheese in the pastry case. Sprinkle with oregano and olives and season to taste. Bake in a preheated oven for 25 minutes until the pastry is golden. Serve warm.

Roast vegetable & feta tart

Feta cheese, the best known Greek cheese, is made from ewes' milk. Its distinctive flavour goes well with these Mediterranean vegetables. Serve warm or cold.

PREPARATION TIME: 25 minutes, plus chilling

COOKING TIME: 45 minutes

OVEN TEMPERATURE: 200°C (400°F), Gas Mark 6

SERVES 6

Pastry:

125 g (4 oz) self-raising flour

50 g (2 oz) oatmeal

75 g (3 oz) chilled butter, diced

3 tablespoons cold water

Filling:

1 aubergine, sliced

1 red pepper, cored, deseeded and cut into thick strips

1 onion, cut into wedges

2 courgettes, cut into thick slices

3 tomatoes, halved

2 garlic cloves, chopped

3 tablespoons olive oil

4 small rosemary sprigs

125 g (4 oz) feta cheese, crumbled

2 tablespoons grated Parmesan cheese

salt and pepper

1 Make the pastry. Mix the flour and oatmeal then rub in the butter. Add the water and mix to a firm dough. Knead briefly, then chill for 30 minutes.

2 Make the filling. Mix all the vegetables in a roasting tin. Add the garlic, oil and rosemary and season to taste. Turn the mixture to coat the vegetables evenly and roast for 35 minutes.

3 Meanwhile, roll out the pastry and line a 23 cm (9 inch) dish. Bake blind for 15 minutes. Remove the paper and beans or foil and return to the oven for 5 minutes.

4 Fill the pastry case with the vegetables, arrange the feta on top and sprinkle with Parmesan. Return to the oven for 10 minutes.

Roast vegetable & feta tart

Courgette & red pepper tart

Serve this colourful tart warm or cold for lunch with a salad of crunchy leaves. Using fresh paprika will enhance both the colour and flavour of the pastry.

PREPARATION TIME: 35 minutes, plus chilling

COOKING TIME: 40 minutes

OVEN TEMPERATURE: 200°C (400°F), Gas Mark 6, then 180°C (350°F), Gas Mark 4

SERVES 6

Pastry:

175 g (6 oz) plain flour

1 teaspoon paprika

75 g (3 oz) chilled butter, diced

Filling:

2 tablespoons olive oil

2 red peppers, cored, deseeded and chopped

375 g (12 oz) courgettes, trimmed

2 eggs, beaten

300 ml (½ pint) milk

50 g (2 oz) mature Cheddar cheese, grated

salt and pepper

1 Sift the flour and paprika into a bowl. Add the butter and rub in with the fingertips until the mixture resembles fine breadcrumbs. Add enough cold water to mix to a firm dough. Turn out the dough on to a lightly floured surface and knead briefly. Chill for 30 minutes.

2 Roll out the pastry and line a 23 cm (9 inch) pie dish. Cut the trimmings into leaf shapes (*see page* 12) and stick them around the rim of the tart with a little water. Chill the pastry case for 30 minutes, then bake blind in a preheated oven for 15 minutes. Remove the paper and beans or foil and set the pastry case aside. Lower the oven temperature to 180°C (350°F), Gas Mark 4.

3 Make the filling. Heat the oil in a frying pan and cook the peppers gently until soft. Season to taste with salt and pepper and purée in a food processor or blender. Alternatively, press the peppers through a sieve. Cut the courgettes into ribbons. Cook them in a saucepan of salted boiling water for 2 minutes, then drain and refresh under cold water. Drain again and pat dry with kitchen paper.

4 Beat the eggs, milk and cheese in a bowl and season to taste with salt and pepper. Spread the pepper purée over the base of the tart. Arrange the courgette ribbons evenly over the top and pour over the cheese sauce. Bake for 25 minutes until the filling is set and golden brown.

Tarte au fromage

This hot soufflé cheesecake is a variation of a classic French supper dish. The sauce can be prepared in advance – cover and chill until required. Serve the tart with a crisp green salad.

PREPARATION TIME: 30 minutes, plus chilling

COOKING TIME: 50 minutes

OVEN TEMPERATURE: 190°C (375°F), Gas Mark 5, then 200°C (400°F), Gas Mark 6

SERVES 4

250 g (8 oz) shortcrust pastry

50 g (2 oz) butter

50 g (2 oz) plain flour

300 ml (½ pint) milk, warmed

250 g (8 oz) Lancashire cheese, grated

6 eggs, separated

2 tablespoons snipped chives, plus extra to garnish

1 tablespoon chopped parsley, plus extra to garnish

½ teaspoon Tabasco sauce or to taste

salt and pepper

1 Make the pastry (*see page* 14). Roll it out and line a deep 20 cm (8 inch) loose-based cake tin. Chill the pastry case for 30 minutes, then bake blind in a pre-heated oven for 15 minutes. Remove the paper and beans or foil and return the tart to the oven for a further 5 minutes. Leave to cool in the cake tin.

2 Make the filling. Melt the butter in a saucepan, blend in the flour and cook over a low heat for 2–3 minutes, stirring all the time. Gradually pour in the milk, beating continuously. Draw off the heat and allow to cool slightly.

3 Beat in the grated cheese and the egg yolks, one at a time. Return to a gentle heat and stir until the cheese has melted. Season to taste with salt and pepper and stir in the chives, parsley and Tabasco.

4 Whisk the egg whites in a bowl until they form stiff peaks and gently fold them into the cheese mixture. Pour the mixture immediately into the cooked pastry case. Bake in a preheated oven, 200°C (400°F), Gas Mark 6, for 30 minutes until well risen and golden. Carefully remove the pastry case from the tin, scatter chopped parsley and chives over the top and serve immediately.

Beetroot & Camembert tart

Do not trim the roots of the beetroots too close to the top of the globe before cooking them, and peel them once cooked so that they do not lose their rich red colour.

PREPARATION TIME: 15 minutes

COOKING TIME: 35–40 minutes

OVEN TEMPERATURE: 200°C (400°F), Gas Mark 6

SERVES 6–8

25 g (1 oz) butter

2 tablespoons honey

3 red onions, thinly sliced

300 ml (½ pint) red wine

500 g (1 lb) cooked beetroot, each beet cut into 6 segments

3 tablespoons chopped thyme, plus sprigs to garnish

375g (12 oz) puff pastry, defrosted if frozen

150 g (5 oz) Camembert, cut into wedges

salt and pepper

1 Melt the butter and honey in a large sauté pan. Add the onions and cook over a medium heat until soft. Add the red wine, season well with salt and pepper and leave to simmer until the mixture has reduced by at least half.

2 Add the beetroot and continue to simmer until the liquid is thick and glossy. Remove from the heat, stir in half the thyme and leave to cool slightly.

3 Make the pastry (*see pages 17–18*). Roll it out and put it on a prepared baking sheet. Use a sharp knife to score a line around the edge, about 2.5 cm (1 inch) in from the sides; do not cut right through the pastry.

4 Spoon the filling on to the pastry making sure you don't go over the border mark. Scatter the cheese slices and the remaining thyme over the top. Bake for 20–25 minutes until the pastry has risen and the cheese is bubbling. Garnish with fresh thyme sprigs.

Sardine tart with a lemon chermoula

Make the chermoula before you prepare the pastry so that the flavours of the sauce have time to develop. Serve the tart hot with fresh green vegetables.

PREPARATION TIME: 25 minutes

COOKING TIME: 40 minutes

OVEN TEMPERATURE: 200°C (400°F), Gas Mark 6

SERVES 4

375 g (12 oz) puff pastry, defrosted if frozen

½ egg, beaten

25 g (1 oz) breadcrumbs

5 sardines, heads, tails and backbones removed

1 beef tomato, halved and thickly sliced

Lemon chermoula:

½ red onion, finely chopped

2 garlic cloves, crushed

3 small preserved lemons, pulp removed and finely chopped

grated rind of 1 lemon and 1 tablespoon of juice

4 tablespoons chopped coriander

4 tablespoons chopped parsley

1 teaspoon paprika

1 teaspoon cumin

½ teaspoon cayenne pepper

4 tablespoons olive oil

salt and pepper

1 Make the chermoula. Mix all the ingredients together in a bowl, season well with salt and pepper then leave to stand.

2 Make the pastry (*see pages* 17–18). Roll it out to 23 x 18 cm (9 x 7 inch) rectangle and put it on a prepared baking sheet. Use a sharp knife to score a mark all the way round the edge, about 2.5 cm (1 inch) in from the sides; do not cut right through the pastry. Brush the pastry with beaten egg and bake in a preheated oven for 15 minutes until risen. Push down the centre piece leaving the border intact. Brush the base of the tart with beaten egg while the pastry is still hot.

3 Sprinkle the base with the breadcrumbs then spoon over half the chermoula mixture. Arrange rows of sardines and sliced tomatoes alternately down the length of the tart base.

4 Top with the remaining chermoula and bake for 25 minutes until the sardines are cooked and the sides of the tart are golden.

Crunchy fish pie

You can use any fish you like in this favourite pie, but take care that you don't overcook it or the flesh will become rubbery and the delicate flavour will be lost.

PREPARATION TIME: 30 minutes, plus chilling

COOKING TIME: 50 minutes

OVEN TEMPERATURE: 200°C (400°F), Gas Mark 6

SERVES 4 as a main course or 6 as a starter

175 g (6 oz) **shortcrust pastry**

200 g (7 oz) **skinned cod fillet**

200 g (7 oz) **undyed smoked haddock fillet**

250 ml (8 fl oz) **milk**

1 **bay leaf**

5 **spring onions, chopped**

200 g (7 oz) **shelled raw prawns**

75 ml (3 fl oz) **double cream**

25 g (1 oz) **plain flour**

25 g (1 oz) **butter**

3 tablespoons **chopped parsley**

salt and pepper

Crumble topping:

25 g (1 oz) **butter**

100 g (3½ oz) **coarse breadcrumbs**

3 tablespoons **chopped parsley**

1 Make the pastry (*see page* 14). Roll it out and line a 20 cm (8 inch) tart tin. Chill the pastry case for 30 minutes, then bake blind in a preheated oven for 15 minutes. Remove the paper and beans or foil and return to the oven for a further 5 minutes.

2 Put the fish, milk and bay leaf in a sauté pan and bring to a gentle boil. Simmer for 3 minutes, remove from the heat, cover with a lid and leave until cold. Strain the liquid into a jug, discard the bay leaf and set aside. Flake the fish into large pieces and put them in the tart case with the spring onions and prawns.

3 Put the reserved milk and the cream in a saucepan with the flour and butter. Stir constantly over a low heat until the butter has melted. Continue to stir until the sauce thickens and reaches boiling point. Allow to simmer for 2–3 minutes, then remove from the heat and stir in the chopped parsley. Season well with salt and pepper and pour over the fish.

4 Make the topping. Melt the butter in a frying pan and gently fry the breadcrumbs for 2–3 minutes until they are light golden in colour. Add the parsley and spoon over the top of the tart. Bake the pie in a preheated oven for 20 minutes until the top is golden and the sauce starts to bubble around the sides. Leave to cool slightly before serving.

Quiche Lorraine
Although this famous dish is often made with cheese and onions, in the traditional recipe the pastry case is filled with bacon, eggs and cream. Serve the quiche warm or cold.

PREPARATION TIME: 20 minutes, plus chilling

COOKING TIME: 55–60 minutes

OVEN TEMPERATURE: 200°C (400°F), Gas Mark 6, then 180°C (350°F), Gas Mark 4

SERVES 4–6

175 g (6 oz) rich shortcrust pastry

175 g (6 oz) rindless smoked back bacon

250 ml (8 fl oz) single cream

2 eggs, beaten

grated nutmeg

salt and pepper

1 Make the pastry (*see page* 15). Roll it out and line a 20 cm (8 inch) tart tin. Chill the pastry case for 30 minutes, then bake blind in a preheated oven for 15 minutes. Remove the paper and beans or foil and return the pastry case to the oven for a further 10 minutes.

2 Make the filling. Grill the bacon until crisp, then drain it on kitchen paper and crumble or cut it into pieces.

3 Beat the cream and eggs in a bowl with the grated nutmeg and season to taste with salt and pepper. Sprinkle the bacon over the case and pour the cream and egg filling over the top.

4 Put the tart tin on a baking sheet and bake in a preheated oven, 180°C (350°F), Gas Mark 4, for 30–35 minutes until the filling is just set and the pastry is golden brown.

Mushroom tart with smoked bacon & thyme

When you are arranging the mushrooms, you may need to overlap them slightly so that they fit neatly. Serve warm with a tomato salad.

PREPARATION TIME: 25 minutes, plus chilling

COOKING TIME: 50 minutes

OVEN TEMPERATURE: 200°C (400°F), Gas Mark 6

SERVES 4

300 g (10 oz) shortcrust pastry

5 large field mushrooms

2 tablespoons chopped thyme

2 tablespoons olive oil

250 g (8 oz) smoked streaky bacon, chopped

1 onion, roughly chopped

3 eggs, beaten

200 ml (7 fl oz) double cream

salt and pepper

thyme sprigs, to garnish

1 Make the pastry (*see page* 14). Roll it out and line a 35 x 12 cm (14 x 5 inch) fluted tart tin. Chill the pastry case for 30 minutes and bake blind in a preheated oven for 10 minutes. Remove the paper and beans or foil and return the pastry case to the oven for a further 10 minutes.

2 Put the mushrooms in a roasting tin, sprinkle over half the chopped thyme and drizzle with 1 tablespoon of olive oil. Cook in the oven for 12 minutes, then remove and leave to cool.

3 Heat the remaining oil in a frying pan. Add the bacon and onion and cook over a medium high heat for 5 minutes until cooked and lightly golden. Spoon over the base of the tart.

4 Beat together the eggs, cream and remaining thyme, season to taste with salt and pepper and pour the mixture into the pastry case. Arrange the mushrooms down the centre of the tart, overlapping them slightly. Bake the tart in a preheated oven for 25–30 minutes until it is coloured on top and set in the centre. Garnish with thyme sprigs.

Lentil, bacon, spinach & Taleggio tart

Taleggio is an Italian cheese, made from cow's milk. It has a pale pink rind and a soft, creamy texture.

PREPARATION TIME: 20 minutes, plus chilling

COOKING TIME: 1 hour

OVEN TEMPERATURE: 200°C (400°F), Gas Mark 6

SERVES 6

300 g (10 oz) shortcrust pastry

100 g (3½ oz) red lentils

1 tablespoon olive oil

250 g (8 oz) streaky bacon, chopped

225 g (7½ oz) baby spinach

3 eggs

2 tablespoons sage, plus a few leaves for garnish

200 ml (7 fl oz) crème fraîche

100 g (3½ oz) Taleggio cheese, cut into cubes

6 cherry tomatoes, halved

salt and pepper

sage leaves, to garnish

1 Make the pastry (*see page* 14). Roll it out and line a 23 cm (9 inch) tart tin. Chill the pastry case for 15 minutes, then bake blind in a preheated oven for 15 minutes. Remove the paper and beans or foil and return to the oven for a further 5 minutes.

2 Meanwhile, cook the lentils in salted boiling water for 10 minutes. Drain and leave to cool slightly. Heat the oil in a frying pan and cook the bacon for 6–7 minutes until golden and crisp.

3 Steam the baby spinach for 1–2 minutes, drain in a sieve and squeeze out as much liquid as possible using the back of a spoon. Roughly chop the spinach.

4 Fill the tart base with the spinach, bacon and lentils. Beat the eggs, sage and crème fraîche and season with black pepper. Pour into the tart and top with the cheese and tomatoes. Bake in a preheated oven for 40 minutes until the filling is firm and golden. Garnish with sage.

Lentil, bacon, spinach & Taleggio tart

Mediterranean salami & olive tart *Use good-quality Italian salami in this recipe to give an authentic flavour of the Mediterranean. Serve the tart warm with a salad of fresh, crisp leaves.*

PREPARATION TIME: 15 minutes, plus rising

COOKING TIME: about 30 minutes

OVEN TEMPERATURE: 220°C (425°F), Gas Mark 7

SERVES 4–6

Pastry:

250 g (8 oz) strong white flour

1 teaspoon easy-blend yeast

1 teaspoon salt

150 ml (¼ pint) hand-hot water

1 tablespoon olive oil

Filling:

250 g (8 oz) can chopped tomatoes

1 tablespoon tomato purée

2 teaspoons dried oregano

125 g (4 oz) sliced salami

75 g (3 oz) black olives, pitted

salt and pepper

1 Mix the flour, yeast and salt in a bowl. Add the water and oil and mix quickly to a soft dough. Turn out on a lightly floured surface and knead for 5 minutes. Put the dough in an oiled polythene bag, tie the top loosely and leave to rise for 30 minutes.

2 Make the filling. Combine the chopped tomatoes and tomato purée in a small saucepan. Add 1 teaspoon of the oregano and season to taste with salt and pepper. Bring the tomato mixture to the boil, stirring, then lower the heat and simmer for about 5 minutes until thickened. Leave to cool.

3 Roll out the pastry and line a 33 x 23 cm (13 x 9 inch) greased Swiss roll tin. Spread with the tomato mixture and arrange the salami slices on top. Sprinkle with the olives and remaining oregano.

4 Bake in a preheated oven for 20–25 minutes until the pastry edges are crisp and golden brown.

Mexican chilli bean tart

When you are removing the seeds and cutting the flesh of chillies, take care that you do not accidentally touch your lips or eyes, and wash your hands thoroughly afterwards.

PREPARATION TIME: 20 minutes, plus chilling

COOKING TIME: 60 minutes

OVEN TEMPERATURE: 200°C (400°F), Gas Mark 6

SERVES 6

300 g (10 oz) shortcrust pastry

500 g (1 lb) minced beef

1 onion, finely chopped

1 red chilli, deseeded and finely chopped

1 garlic clove, crushed

30 g (1¼ oz) packet taco seasoning mix

400 g (13 oz) can chopped tomatoes

4 tablespoons vegetable stock

400 g (13 oz) can mixed beans, rinsed and drained

50 g (2 oz) nachos, broken slightly

100 g (3½ oz) Cheddar cheese, grated

2 tablespoons chopped coriander leaves

To serve:

soured cream

tomato salsa

1 Make the pastry (*see page* 14). Roll it out and line a 23 cm (9 inch) fluted tart tin. Chill the pastry case for 30 minutes, then bake blind in a preheated oven for 15 minutes. Remove the paper and beans or foil and return to the oven for a further 5 minutes.

2 Put the mince in a nonstick pan and cook for 5 minutes, stirring to break up the lumps of meat, until it is evenly browned. Add the onion, chilli, garlic and taco mix and continue to cook for 2–3 minutes. Add the tomatoes and stock and season to taste with salt and pepper. Bring to the boil and simmer for 10 minutes. Stir in the mixed beans and cook for a further 2 minutes until the sauce thickens.

3 Pour the sauce into the tart case. Mix together the nachos, cheese and coriander and put them on top of the sauce.

4 Bake in a preheated oven for 20 minutes until the cheese has melted and the nachos have coloured. Leave to stand for about 15 minutes before serving with soured cream and tomato salsa.

Italian sausage & onion tart

Keep the paper-thin sheets of filo pastry covered with clingfilm or a damp cloth until you are ready to use them, to prevent them from drying out.

PREPARATION TIME: 20 minutes

COOKING TIME: 1 hour

OVEN TEMPERATURE: 180°C (350°F), Gas Mark 4

SERVES 4

3 tablespoons olive oil

6 Italian sausages

2 red onions, cut into wedges

6 sheets filo pastry

100 g (3½ oz) mascarpone cheese

50 g (2 oz) Roquefort cheese

3 large eggs

2 tablespoons milk

1 tablespoon wholegrain mustard

chives, to garnish

1 Heat 1 tablespoon of the oil in a frying pan and cook the sausages and onions over a medium heat for about 15 minutes until they are browned and cooked. Leave to one side.

2 Brush the filo sheets with the remaining oil. Line a 35 x 12 cm (14 x 5 inch) loose-based tart tin with the pastry, overlapping and overhanging the sheets. Bunch up the overhanging filo to make a rim around the sides. Bake in a preheated oven for 10 minutes or until the base is dry. Leave the oven on.

3 Whisk together the mascarpone, Roquefort, eggs, milk and mustard to make a smooth mixture. Pour it into the base of the tart.

4 Arrange the sausages and onion wedges evenly over the batter. Bake for 30–35 minutes until golden and set. Serve warm, garnished with fresh chives.

Italian sausage & onion tart

Potato & salami tart with red pesto

Ready-made pesto in a range of flavours and colours is widely available in supermarkets, but if you prefer, use your favourite recipe in this tart.

PREPARATION TIME: 10 minutes, plus chilling

COOKING TIME: 50–60 minutes

OVEN TEMPERATURE: 200°C (400°F), Gas Mark 6

SERVES 4

475 g (15 oz) potatoes

300 g (10 oz) puff pastry, defrosted if frozen

65 g (2½ oz) ready-made red pesto

1½ tablespoons crème fraîche

75 g (3 oz) salami slices

40 g (1½ oz) melted butter

1 Cook the potatoes in a pan of salted boiling water for 20–25 minutes. Drain, leave them to cool, then cut them into 1 cm (½ inch) slices.

2 Make the pastry (*see pages* 17–18). Roll it out to about 5 mm (¼ inch) thick, put it on a prepared baking sheet and chill for 30 minutes. Cut the pastry into a 24 cm (9½ inch) disc and use a sharp knife to score a border about 2.5 cm (1 inch) in from the edge all the way round; do not cut right through the pastry.

3 Mix the pesto with the crème fraîche and spread the mixture over the pastry, keeping inside the border. Arrange the potato and salami slices alternately over the pesto base.

4 Brush the tart with melted butter and bake it in a preheated oven for 30–35 minutes until the pastry is risen and golden.

Sweet potato, chorizo & red pepper tart

Chorizo is a Spanish pork sausage, traditionally flavoured with red peppers. It is a wonderful complement to the sweet potato.

PREPARATION TIME: 30 minutes

COOKING TIME: 50–60 minutes

OVEN TEMPERATURE: 200°C (400°F), Gas Mark 6

SERVES 4

750 g (1½ lb) sweet potato, cut into 2.5 cm (1 inch) cubes

1 large red pepper, cored, deseeded and cut into 2.5 cm (1 inch) cubes

3 garlic cloves, left in their skins

2 tablespoons olive oil

150 g (5 oz) chorizo, cut into 1 cm (½ inch) cubes

125 g (4 oz) ricotta cheese

100 g (3½ oz) Cheddar cheese, grated

2 tablespoons crème fraîche

2 egg yolks

375 g (12 oz) shortcrust pastry

1 egg, beaten, to glaze

3 rosemary sprigs

salt and pepper

1 Put the sweet potato, red pepper and garlic in a roasting dish. Drizzle with olive oil, season with salt and pepper and bake in a preheated oven for 15 minutes. Add the chorizo and bake for a further 5–10 minutes or until the vegetables are slightly golden. Remove and leave to cool.

2 Push the garlic pulp out of the skins and put in a bowl with the ricotta, Cheddar, crème fraîche and egg yolks. Beat together to make a smooth mixture.

3 Make the pastry (*see page* 14). Roll it out to a 30 cm (12 inch) circle and put it on a prepared baking sheet. Brush the pastry with beaten egg. Spoon the ricotta mixture into the centre of the pastry, leaving a 7 cm (3 inch) border around the sides. Place the roasted vegetables and chorizo on top of the ricotta mixture.

4 Fold in the pastry border so that it partly overlaps the filling. Brush the sides with more beaten egg. Scatter with rosemary sprigs and season to taste with salt and pepper. Bake in a preheated oven for 30–35 minutes until the pastry is golden.

Dolcelatte & leek galette
Creamy blue dolcelatte has a smooth, mild flavour, which is ideal in rich sauces. Do not overcook the leeks, which can become tough and unpalatable.

PREPARATION TIME: 15 minutes

COOKING TIME: 20–22 minutes

OVEN TEMPERATURE: 220°C (425°F), Gas Mark 7

SERVES 4

8 thin leeks

300 g (10 oz) puff pastry, defrosted if frozen

50 ml (2 fl oz) crème fraîche

1 teaspoon cayenne pepper

1 tablespoon wholegrain mustard

50 g (2 oz) dolcelatte cheese, crumbled

1 egg, beaten

salt and pepper

chopped parsley, to garnish (optional)

1 Trim the leeks to 20 cm (8 inches) and put them in a frying pan. Pour in enough boiling water to cover them and bring back to the boil. Reduce the heat, cover the pan and simmer for 5–7 minutes. Drain the leeks and set aside.

2 Make the pastry (*see pages* 17–18). Roll it out to about 25 cm (10 inches) square and put it on a prepared baking sheet. Use a sharp knife to score all the way round the pastry 3.5 cm (1½ inches) in from the edge; do not cut right through the pastry.

3 Pat the leeks dry with kitchen paper to remove any excess moisture and arrange them on the pastry inside the border.

4 Mix together the crème fraîche, cayenne, mustard and cheese and gently spread the mixture over the leeks. Season well with salt and pepper and cook in a preheated oven for 15 minutes or until the pastry has risen and the border has browned. Cut the galette into quarters and sprinkle each portion with chopped parsley, if using. Serve immediately.

Asparagus, Parmesan & egg tart
This tart makes good use of a small amount of asparagus. Use young, thin spears and cut off the thick, woody section at the base.

PREPARATION TIME: 35 minutes. plus chilling

COOKING TIME: 40–45 minutes

OVEN TEMPERATURE: 200°C (400°F), Gas Mark 6, then 180°C (350°F), Gas Mark 4

SERVES 4

175 g (6 oz) shortcrust pastry

175 g (6 oz) thin asparagus spears

5 eggs

150 ml (¼ pint) single cream

25 g (1 oz) grated Parmesan cheese

salt and pepper

1 Make the pastry (*see page 14*). Roll it out and line a 20 cm (8 inch) tart tin. Chill the pastry case for 30 minutes, then bake blind in a preheated oven for 15 minutes. Remove the paper and beans or foil and return the tart to the oven for a further 10 minutes.

2 Meanwhile, trim the woody ends from the asparagus. Stand the spears upright in a tall saucepan and add salted boiling water to cover all but the tips of the asparagus. Cover the pan and cook for 7–10 minutes, until tender. Drain the asparagus in a colander and refresh under cold running water. Drain again.

3 Beat one of the eggs in a bowl with the cream and season to taste with salt and pepper. Arrange the asparagus in the base of the pastry case. Break each of the remaining eggs in turn into a saucer and carefully slide them into the pastry case.

4 Pour the cream mixture over the eggs, sprinkle with Parmesan and bake the tart in a preheated oven, 180°C (350°F), Gas Mark 4, for 15–20 minutes until the eggs have just set. Serve warm.

Gorgonzola & hazelnut quiche

This rich and creamy tart is packed with leeks. Cooked until just set, it is topped with a layer of toasted whole hazelnuts for extra crunch.

PREPARATION TIME: 30 minutes, plus chilling

COOKING TIME: about 1¼ hours

OVEN TEMPERATURE: 190°C (375°F), Gas Mark 5

SERVES 6–8

50 g (2 oz) butter

1 tablespoon vegetable oil

2 large leeks, thinly sliced

150 ml (¼ pint) whipping cream

150 ml (¼ pint) milk

2 tablespoons chopped flat-leaf parsley

2 eggs, beaten

125 g (4 oz) Gorgonzola cheese, crumbled

75 g (3 oz) whole hazelnuts, lightly toasted

salt and pepper

Pastry:

250 g (8 oz) plain flour

pinch of salt

pinch of cayenne pepper

75 g (3 oz) chilled butter, diced

25 g (1 oz) Cheddar cheese, finely grated

6–8 tablespoons cold water

1 Make the pastry. Put the flour, salt and cayenne pepper in a bowl, add the butter and rub in with your fingertips until the mixture resembles breadcrumbs. Mix in the grated Cheddar. Add enough water to make a soft, pliable pastry, wrap it in clingfilm and chill for 30 minutes.

2 Roll out the pastry and line a deep 20 cm (8 inch) tart tin. Chill the pastry case for 30 minutes and bake blind in a preheated oven for 12 minutes. Remove the paper and beans or foil and return to the oven for a further 5 minutes.

3 Make the filling. Heat the butter and oil in a frying pan and fry the sliced leeks until they are softened and caramelized. Remove from the heat and allow to cool. Beat together the cream, milk, parsley and eggs. Stir the egg mixture into the leeks and season well with salt and pepper. Stir the Gorgonzola into the mixture, then pour it into the pastry case. Smooth the surface, then scatter the hazelnuts over the top.

4 Bake the quiche in a preheated oven for 40–50 minutes or until the egg mixture has just set in the middle. Remove from the oven and allow to cool slightly before serving with a mixed salad.

Onion tarte Tatin
Shallots are related to onions but form a cluster of small bulbs rather than a single one. They have a subtler flavour than onions and are not as pungent as garlic.

PREPARATION TIME: 30 minutes, plus chilling
COOKING TIME: 30–35 minutes
OVEN TEMPERATURE: 200°C (400°F), Gas Mark 6
SERVES 4–6

Pastry:

175 g (6 oz) self-raising wholemeal flour

75 g (3 oz) chilled butter, diced

2 tablespoons chopped parsley

2 teaspoons chopped thyme

2–3 tablespoons lemon juice

Filling:

500 g (1 lb) shallots, peeled

25 g (1 oz) butter

2 tablespoons olive oil

2 teaspoons muscovado sugar

salt and pepper

1 Sift the flour into a bowl and rub in the butter until the mixture resembles breadcrumbs. Stir in the herbs and lemon juice and mix to a firm dough. Knead briefly, then chill for 30 minutes.

2 Make the filling. Boil the shallots for 10 minutes and drain well. Heat the butter and oil in an ovenproof frying pan, and gently fry the shallots, stirring, for about 10 minutes until they start to colour. Sprinkle over the sugar, season to taste with salt and pepper and cook gently for 5 minutes until well coloured.

3 Roll out the dough to a round, a little larger than the pan. Support the dough on the rolling pin and lay it over the shallots, tucking the edges of the pastry down the side of the pan.

4 Bake the tart in a preheated oven for 20–25 minutes until the pastry is crisp. Leave the tart to cool for 5 minutes, then put a large plate over the pan and invert the tart on to it. Serve warm or cold.

Roast root vegetable tarte Tatin
This savoury version of the classic sweet tarte Tatin was inspired by the caramelization of roasted root vegetables and the simplicity of the crisp pastry base.

PREPARATION TIME: 15 minutes, plus chilling

COOKING TIME: 50–55 minutes

OVEN TEMPERATURE: 220°C (425°F), Gas Mark 7

SERVES 6

3 tablespoons olive oil

175 g (6 oz) carrots, cut into 2.5 cm (1 inch) chunks

175 g (6 oz) turnips, cut into 2.5 cm (1 inch) chunks

175 g (6 oz) parsnips, cut into 2.5 cm (1 inch) chunks

175 g (6 oz) shallots, halved if large

1 teaspoon coriander seeds, finely ground

1 teaspoon fennel seeds, finely ground

4 garlic cloves, peeled

175 g (6 oz) leeks, cut into 2.5 cm (1 inch) chunks

375 g (12 oz) puff pastry, defrosted if frozen

Caramel:

20 g (¾ oz) butter

40 g (1½ oz) sugar

1 tablespoon red wine vinegar

25 ml (1 fl oz) water

1 Heat the oil in a roasting tin and add the carrots, turnips, parsnips, shallots and spices. Toss over a high heat until lightly coloured, then transfer to a preheated oven for 20 minutes. Add the garlic and cook for 10 minutes. Add the leeks and cook for a further 10 minutes or until the vegetables are tender and a rich brown colour.

2 Meanwhile, make the pastry (*see pages 17–18*). Roll it out and cut it into six 11 cm (4½ inch) circles. Cover and chill until required.

3 Make the caramel. Combine all the ingredients in a frying pan, bring to the boil, shaking the pan and stirring until the sugar dissolves, and let the mixture bubble until it turns a deep golden caramel. (It will turn pink and frothy first.) Keep shaking the pan and drawing a spoon across the centre to disperse the heat. Quickly pour the caramel into the centre of six shallow 7 cm (3 inch) heavy pie tins, spreading it over their bases if you can. It may set immediately but will liquefy in the oven.

4 Arrange the vegetables over the caramel. Put the pastry discs over them, tucking in the edges so that they lie on top of the vegetables inside the tins. Set the pies on a baking sheet and bake for 10–15 minutes until the pastry is crisp and golden. Cool for a few minutes, then invert on to warmed plates, handling the tarts carefully as the hot juices may run out. Serve the tarts hot, pastry side down.

Onion, raisin & pine nut tart *The slightly resinous, spicy flavour of pine nuts combines perfectly with the mozzarella in this simple tart, which makes a delicious lunchtime treat.*

PREPARATION TIME: 25 minutes

COOKING TIME: 35–40 minutes

OVEN TEMPERATURE: 200°C (400°F), Gas Mark 6

SERVES 4

75 g (3 oz) butter

2 teaspoons mustard seeds

150 g (5 oz) plain flour

125 g (4 oz) mashed potato

2 tablespoons olive oil

2 onions, thinly sliced

125 g (4 oz) mozzarella cheese, sliced

25 g (1 oz) pine nuts

25 g (1 oz) raisins

salt and pepper

1 Heat 25 g (1 oz) of the butter in a frying pan and fry the mustard seeds until they start to pop. Cut the remaining butter into cubes and rub it into the flour in a bowl. Stir in the mashed potato and the mustard seeds with the melted butter. Season to taste with salt and pepper and mix to a soft dough.

2 Press the dough out to form a 25 cm (10 inch) square and put it on a prepared baking sheet. Neatly pinch the edges to make a rim.

3 Heat the oil in a frying pan, add the onions and fry for about 5 minutes until soft and lightly browned. Arrange the mozzarella slices evenly over the pastry base, then scatter the pine nuts and raisins over the top. Cover with the onions and sprinkle with salt and pepper.

4 Bake the tart in a preheated oven for 25–30 minutes until the pastry is golden brown. Serve hot.

Butternut squash & Jarlsberg tart with oregano oil

Jarlsberg is a soft Norwegian cheese with a slightly nutty flavour. If you cannot find Jarlsberg, use Emmenthal instead.

PREPARATION TIME: 20 minutes, plus chilling

COOKING TIME: 1 hour

OVEN TEMPERATURE: 180°C (350°F), Gas Mark 4

SERVES 6

300 g (10 oz) shortcrust pastry

1 tablespoon sun-dried tomato paste

1 kg (2 lb) butternut squash, peeled, halved and sliced; about 625 g (1¼ lb) prepared weight

250 g (8 oz) Jarlsberg cheese, rind removed and thinly sliced

2 tablespoons chopped oregano

3 tablespoons olive oil

6 thin slices Parma ham

1 Make the pastry (*see page* 14). Roll it out and line a 25 cm (10 inch) fluted tart tin. Spread the tomato paste over the base and chill for 30 minutes.

2 Arrange the slices of butternut in the tart, overlapping each slice with the next. Push the slices of cheese between the slices of butternut squash.

3 Stir the oregano into the oil and use half to brush over the tart. Bake the tart in a preheated oven for 30 minutes. Remove from the oven.

4 Loosely arrange the slices of Parma ham over the tart, brush with the remaining herb oil and return to the oven for a further 30 minutes.

Butternut squash & Jarlsberg tart with oregano oil

Smoked haddock & spinach tart
Smoked haddock gives this simple tart a delicious savoury flavour. Serve it warm for supper with new potatoes and a chicory and orange salad.

PREPARATION TIME: 20 minutes, plus chilling

COOKING TIME: 40 minutes

OVEN TEMPERATURE: 200°C (400°F), Gas Mark 6, then 190°C (375°F), Gas Mark 5

SERVES 4–6

Pastry:

75 g (3 oz) wholemeal flour

75 g (3 oz) plain flour

75 g (3 oz) chilled butter, diced

2–3 tablespoons iced water

Filling:

350 g (11½ oz) smoked haddock fillet

300 ml (½ pint) milk

125 g (4 oz) frozen leaf spinach, defrosted

40 g (1½ oz) butter

25 g (1 oz) plain flour

2 eggs, beaten

75 g (3 oz) mature Cheddar cheese, grated

salt and pepper

1 Mix the flours in a bowl, add the butter and rub in with the fingertips until the mixture resembles breadcrumbs. Stir in enough water to make a firm dough. Knead the dough briefly and chill for 30 minutes. Roll it out and line a deep 20 cm (8 inch) tart tin. Bake the pastry case blind in a preheated oven for 15 minutes.

2 Meanwhile, make the filling. Put the haddock in a pan and pour over the milk. Bring to the boil, then cover the pan, lower the heat and cook gently for about 10 minutes until the haddock is tender and flakes easily. Use a slotted spoon to remove the fish from the pan. Strain the cooking liquid into a jug. Skin and flake the fish.

3 Press the spinach in a sieve to extract as much liquid as possible. Heat the butter in a pan until bubbling, stir in the flour and cook for 1 minute. Gradually stir in the reserved cooking liquid until the sauce is thick and smooth.

4 Let the sauce cool for 5 minutes, then stir in the spinach, eggs and haddock. Add 50 g (2 oz) of the cheese and season to taste with salt and pepper. Stir well and pour into the pastry case. Sprinkle over the remaining cheese and bake in a preheated oven, 190°C (375°F), Gas Mark 5, for about 25 minutes.

Salmon tart with wholegrain mustard & rocket

Rocket is related to mustard and watercress; the young leaves have a sharp, peppery flavour that is immediately recognizable.

PREPARATION TIME: 20 minutes, plus chilling

COOKING TIME: 45–50 minutes

OVEN TEMPERATURE: 200°C (400°F), Gas Mark 6

SERVES 4

Pastry:

225 g (7½ oz) plain flour

100 g (3½ oz) butter

grated rind of 1 lemon

1 tablespoon cracked black pepper

4 tablespoons iced water

Filling:

300 g (10 oz) salmon fillet or loin, skinned and all bones removed

250 ml (8 fl oz) milk

50 g (2 oz) rocket, plus extra leaves to garnish

3 eggs, beaten

3 tablespoons wholegrain mustard

5 spring onions, finely chopped

1 Put the flour, butter, lemon rind and black pepper in a food processor and blitz until the mixture resembles fine breadcrumbs. Add the water and pulse a few times until the mixture comes together. Cover with clingfilm and chill for 1 hour.

2 Roll out the pastry and line a deep 20 cm (8 inch) fluted tart tin. Chill the pastry case for 30 minutes, then bake blind in a preheated oven for 15 minutes. Remove the paper and beans or foil and return to the oven for a further 5 minutes.

3 Poach the salmon in the milk for 5 minutes until cooked. Leave to cool slightly. Put the chopped rocket in the base of the pastry case. Remove the salmon from the milk and strain and reserve the cooking liquid. Break the salmon into bite-sized pieces and arrange them over the rocket.

4 Beat together the eggs, mustard, spring onions and poaching milk and pour over the salmon. Bake in a preheated oven for 25–30 minutes until golden and firm. Garnish with rocket leaves.

Prawn & courgette tart

Use a young courgette with a dark green, glossy skin. As they age, the skins of courgettes become duller and the flavour is less intense.

PREPARATION TIME: 25 minutes, plus chilling

COOKING TIME: 40 minutes

OVEN TEMPERATURE: 200°C (400°F), Gas Mark 6, then 190°C (375°F), Gas Mark 5

SERVES 4–6

175 g (6 oz) shortcrust pastry

40 g (1½ oz) butter

1 courgette, cut into matchsticks

25 g (1 oz) plain flour

300 ml (½ pint) hot milk

175 g (6 oz) peeled cooked prawns, defrosted if frozen

2 eggs, beaten

75 g (3 oz) mature Cheddar cheese, grated

salt and pepper

1 Make the pastry (*see page* 14). Roll it out and line a 23 cm (9 inch) tart tin. Chill for 30 minutes, then bake the pastry case blind in a preheated oven for 15 minutes.

2 Make the filling. Melt the butter in a saucepan, add the courgette matchsticks and cook gently for about 5 minutes until softened. Stir in the flour and cook for 1 minute. Gradually stir in the hot milk, cooking until the sauce is thick and smooth.

3 Let the sauce cool slightly, then stir in the prawns and eggs with 50 g (2 oz) of the grated cheese. Season to taste with salt and pepper. Pour the filling into the pastry case and sprinkle with the remaining grated cheese.

4 Bake the tart in a preheated oven, 190°C (375°F), Gas Mark 5, for about 25 minutes until the filling is golden brown. Serve warm.

Prawn & courgette tart

Leek & mussel tart

If you prefer to buy raw mussels you will need about 500 g (1 lb). Scrub them thoroughly and cook in water over a high heat until the shells open. Discard any that remain shut.

PREPARATION TIME: 25 minutes, plus chilling

COOKING TIME: 30 minutes

OVEN TEMPERATURE: 200°C (400°F), Gas Mark 6

SERVES 4–6

175 g (6 oz) rich shortcrust pastry

25 g (1 oz) butter

2 leeks, trimmed, cleaned and sliced

175 g (6 oz) shelled, cooked mussels

3 tablespoons crème fraîche

2 tablespoons dried breadcrumbs

3 tablespoons chopped parsley

1 garlic clove, chopped

2 tablespoons olive oil

salt and pepper

1 Make the pastry (*see page* 15). Roll it out and line a 20 cm (8 inch) tart tin. Chill the pastry case for 30 minutes, then bake blind in a preheated oven for 15 minutes. Remove the paper and beans or foil and return the tart to the oven for a further 10 minutes.

2 Melt the butter in a frying pan and cook the leeks for about 5 minutes until softened and tender. Add the mussels and crème fraîche to the pan. Season to taste with salt and pepper and stir over a gentle heat until warmed through.

3 Mix the breadcrumbs, parsley, garlic and oil in a small bowl.

4 Fill the warm pastry case with the mussel and leek mixture, then sprinkle the breadcrumb mixture over the top. Place under a preheated moderate grill until the crumbs are browned and crisp. Serve the tart warm.

Smoked chicken & wild mushroom tart

Ordinary roast chicken can be used if you prefer, but the combination of wild mushrooms and smoked meat is mouthwateringly good.

PREPARATION TIME: 20 minutes, plus chilling

COOKING TIME: 55–60 minutes

OVEN TEMPERATURE: 200°C (400°F), Gas Mark 6

SERVES 6

375 g (12 oz) shortcrust pastry

1–2 tablespoons olive oil

125 g (4 oz) mixed wild mushrooms

½ a cooked smoked chicken

100 g (3½ oz) sun-blushed tomatoes

100 g (3½ oz) Cheddar cheese, grated

3 eggs

300 ml (½ pint) double cream

2 tablespoons chopped tarragon

1 Make the pastry (*see page* 14). Roll it out and line a 30 x 20 cm (12 x 8 inch) fluted tart tin. Chill the pastry case for 30 minutes, then bake blind in a preheated oven for 15 minutes. Remove the paper and beans or foil and return to the oven for a further 5 minutes.

2 Heat the oil in a frying pan and cook the mushrooms for 3–4 minutes until they are lightly coloured and cooked.

3 Remove the chicken meat from the bones and carcass, cutting the larger pieces into bite-sized chunks. Sprinkle the chicken, tomatoes, mushrooms and cheese into the pastry case.

4 Mix together the eggs, cream and tarragon. Pour over the filling and bake in a preheated oven for 30–35 minutes until golden and set.

Crispy duck tarts
These individual tarts have a distinctly oriental flavour partly because of the hoisin sauce, which is a common ingredient in many South-east Asian dishes. Serve hot or cold.

PREPARATION TIME: 45 minutes, plus chilling

COOKING TIME: 55 minutes

OVEN TEMPERATURE: 200°C (400°F), Gas Mark 6

SERVES 6

375 g (12 oz) puff pastry, defrosted if frozen
beaten egg or milk, to glaze
2 duck legs
6 tablespoons crème fraîche
8 tablespoons hoisin sauce
6 spring onions, thinly sliced
½ cucumber, cut into matchsticks
15 g (½ oz) coriander, leaves

1 Make the pastry (*see pages* 17–18). Cut six 10 cm (4 inch) squares. Make two L-shaped cuts in the pastry 2.5 cm (1 inch) in from the edge, leaving the two opposite corners uncut. Brush the edges of the pastry square with water.

2 Lift up one cut corner and draw it across the pastry to the opposite cut side. Repeat with the other cut side to form a case. Brush the edges of the pastry with egg or milk, prick the base, put on a prepared baking sheet and chill.

3 Prick the duck legs with a fork and place on a rack over a baking tin to catch the fat. Roast for 30 minutes. Leave to cool, then shred the meat and skin from the duck legs.

4 Put the meat a bowl with the crème fraîche and hoisin sauce, mix well and divide among the bases of the prepared tarts. Bake for 25 minutes until the pastry has risen and is golden on top.

5 Mix the spring onion, cucumber and coriander and arrange the mixture on top of the tarts just before serving. The tarts can be eaten hot or cold.

Crispy duck tarts

Potato tart with ham, artichokes & mushrooms

This free-form tart has a moist, scone-like dough, which is perfect for all sorts of savoury toppings.

PREPARATION TIME: 20 minutes

COOKING TIME: 30–40 minutes

OVEN TEMPERATURE: 200°C (400°F), Gas Mark 6

SERVES 4

75 g (3 oz) butter

1 onion, thinly sliced

150 g (5 oz) plain flour

125 g (4 oz) mashed potato

1 tablespoon olive oil

2 shallots, sliced

125 g (4 oz) mushrooms, sliced

125 g (4 oz) cooked ham, cut into strips

175 g (6 oz) drained canned artichoke hearts, sliced

salt and pepper

thyme sprigs, to garnish

1 Melt 25 g (1 oz) of the butter in a saucepan, add the onion and fry until it is softened and lightly browned. Leave to cool slightly.

2 Dice the remaining butter and rub it into the flour in a bowl. Add the onion with the pan juices and the mashed potato and season to taste with salt and pepper. Mix to a soft dough. Press out the dough on a prepared baking sheet to a 23 cm (9 inch) round. Pinch the edges of the dough to make a rim.

3 Heat the oil in a frying pan, add the shallots and fry until they are lightly browned. Add the mushrooms and cook briefly until softened.

4 Scatter the ham and artichokes over the dough, then top with the shallot and mushroom mixture. Season again if wished and bake in a preheated oven for 25–30 minutes until the pastry is golden brown. Serve hot, garnished with thyme sprigs.

Potato tart with ham, artichokes & mushrooms

Mozzarella & tomato tartlets
These tartlets take next to no time to prepare but will make a delicious and filling lunch served with a fresh, crisp salad.

PREPARATION TIME: 15 minutes

COOKING TIME: about 20 minutes

OVEN TEMPERATURE: 200°C (400°F), Gas Mark 6

SERVES 6

250 g (8 oz) puff pastry, defrosted if frozen

beaten egg or milk, to glaze

6 tablespoons sun-dried tomato paste

3 plum tomatoes, deseeded and roughly chopped

125 g (4 oz) mozzarella, roughly diced

8 black olives, pitted and roughly chopped

1 garlic clove, finely chopped

2 tablespoons roughly chopped oregano

1 tablespoon pine nuts

olive oil, to drizzle

salt and pepper

mixed salad leaves, to serve

1 Make the pastry (*see pages* 17–18). Roll it out to 3 mm (⅛ inch) thick. Use a round cutter to stamp out six 12 cm (5 inch) circles and put them on a prepared baking sheet. Use a sharp knife to make a shallow mark 1 cm (½ inch) in from the edge of each round to form a rim; do not cut right through the pastry. Brush the rims with beaten egg or milk.

2 Spread 1 tablespoon of tomato paste over each pastry circle. Mix together the tomatoes, mozzarella, olives, garlic, oregano and pine nuts in a small bowl and season to taste with salt and pepper.

3 Divide this mixture among the pastry circles and drizzle a little olive oil over the tartlets.

4 Bake the tartlets in a preheated oven for 20 minutes or until the pastry has risen and is golden. Serve at once with mixed salad leaves.

Cherry tomato tarts with pesto sauce *Use ready-made pesto or your own favourite recipe in this colourful dish, but make sure it is green to contrast with the brilliant red tomatoes.*

PREPARATION TIME: 10 minutes

COOKING TIME: 18 minutes

OVEN TEMPERATURE: 220°C (425°F), Gas Mark 7

SERVES 4

2 tablespoons olive oil

1 onion, finely chopped

375 g (12 oz) cherry tomatoes

2 garlic cloves, crushed

3 tablespoons sun-dried tomato paste

325 g (11 oz) puff pastry, defrosted if frozen

beaten egg, to glaze

150 g (5 oz) crème fraîche

2 tablespoons ready-made pesto

salt and pepper

basil leaves, to garnish

1 Heat the oil in a frying pan, add the onion and fry until it is beginning to soften. Halve about 150 g (5 oz) of the tomatoes. Remove the pan from the heat, add the garlic and sun-dried tomato paste, then stir in all the tomatoes until they are lightly coated in the sauce.

2 Make the pastry (*see pages* 17–18). Roll it out and cut out four 12 cm (5 inch) rounds using a cutter or small bowl as a guide. Transfer to a prepared baking sheet and use a sharp knife to make a shallow mark 1 cm (½ inch) in from the edge of each round to form a rim; do not cut right through the pastry. Brush the rims with beaten egg.

3 Pile the tomato mixture on to the centres of the pastry cases, making sure the mixture stays within the rims. Bake in a preheated oven for about 15 minutes until the pastry is risen and golden.

4 Meanwhile, lightly mix together the crème fraîche, pesto and salt and pepper in a bowl so that the crème fraîche is streaked with the pesto. Transfer the cooked tartlets to serving plates and spoon over the crème fraîche and pesto sauce. Serve scattered with basil leaves.

Dolcelatte & broad bean tartlets *The inclusion of wholemeal flour in the pastry gives a slightly nutty flavour. Fresh broad beans don't keep well, so use them straight away.*

PREPARATION TIME: 15 minutes, plus chilling

COOKING TIME: 30–40 minutes

OVEN TEMPERATURE: 200°C (400°F), Gas Mark 6

SERVES 4

Pastry:

75 g (3 oz) plain flour

75 g (3 oz) self-raising wholemeal flour

75 g (3 oz) butter, diced

2–3 tablespoons iced water

Filling:

1 red pepper

500 g (1 lb) broad beans, in pods

125 g (4 oz) dolcelatte, crumbled

2 tablespoons single cream

salt and pepper

1 Mix the flours in a bowl. Add the butter and rub in with the fingertips until the mixture resembles fine breadcrumbs. Add just enough water to make a firm dough. Turn out on to a lightly floured surface, knead briefly and chill for 30 minutes.

2 Divide the dough into four and roll out each piece to line a shallow 10 cm (4 inch) tart tin. Chill the pastry cases for 15 minutes. Prick the base of each tartlet several times with a fork, then bake in a preheated oven for 15–20 minutes.

3 Quarter and deseed the pepper, then put the pieces, skin side up, under a hot grill until the skin is charred. Peel off the skin when it is cool enough to handle.

4 Meanwhile, pod the beans and cook in a pan of boiling water for 7–10 minutes until just tender. Drain and slip off the outer skins.

5 Chop the pepper flesh into small dice, combine it with the beans and divide the mixture among the tartlets. Scatter dolcelatte over the vegetables, then pour over the cream. Season to taste with salt and pepper. Bake for 8–10 minutes until the cheese has melted. Serve warm.

Spicy crab tartlets
These dainty tartlets are filled with a wonderful combination of Asian flavours. They are surprisingly easy to make and make excellent party canapés.

PREPARATION TIME: 10–12 minutes plus chilling

COOKING TIME: 10–12 minutes

OVEN TEMPERATURE: 200°C (400°F), Gas Mark 6

MAKES: 12 canapés

375 g (12 oz) **shortcrust pastry**

125 g (4 oz) **fresh white crab meat**

1 **ripe tomato, peeled, deseeded and finely chopped**

1 **small garlic clove, crushed**

2 **tablespoons chopped coriander leaves**

¼–½ **teaspoon ground cayenne**

4 **tablespoons mayonnaise**

dash of lemon juice

salt and pepper

1 Make the pastry (*see page* 14). Roll it out thinly and use a 6 cm (2½ inch) cutter to stamp out 12 circles. Line the sections of a bun tin with the pastry, prick the base of each one with a fork and chill for 15 minutes. Bake in a preheated oven for 10–12 minutes until lightly golden. Leave to cool.

2 Carefully fork through the crab meat to remove any small pieces of cartilage that may remain.

3 Add the tomato, garlic, coriander, cayenne and mayonnaise to the crab. Add a little lemon juice and season to taste with salt and pepper.

4 Fill the tartlet cases with the crab mixture and serve.

Filo tarts with red pepper & pancetta *If you cannot find spicy Italian pancetta use the best quality streaky bacon. Remember to keep the filo pastry covered so that it does not dry out.*

PREPARATION TIME: 10 minutes

COOKING TIME: 36–38 minutes

OVEN TEMPERATURE: 200°C (400°F), Gas Mark 6

SERVES 6

6–8 sheets filo pastry, each cut into three 11 cm (4½ inch) squares

25 g (1 oz) butter, melted

1 tablespoon olive oil

125 g (4 oz) pancetta, diced

1 large red pepper, cored deseeded and roughly chopped

1 red onion, roughly chopped

1 teaspoon hot paprika

100 ml (3½ fl oz) passata

6 eggs

50 g (2 oz) Gruyère cheese, grated

1 Brush the filo squares with melted butter and stick them together at different angles in piles of three so that you end up with six stacks. Push each stack into a 10 cm (4 inch) tart case and bake in a preheated oven for 8–10 minutes.

2 Heat the oil in a frying pan and fry the pancetta, red pepper, onion and paprika for 8 minutes until just cooked through.

3 Remove from the heat and stir in the passata. Divide the mixture among the tart cases, making a well in the centre of each tart.

4 Crack an egg into each well, sprinkle with the cheese and bake in a preheated oven for 20 minutes.

Filo tarts with red pepper & pancetta

Sweet & fruity *Pâte sucrée or rich shortcrust pastry is usually used for sweet tarts, especially for moulded or decorated tarts because the pastry holds its shape well. When cooking sweet pastries, take care never to overcook or leave them in the oven once the pastry has begun to turn golden brown. The sugar in the pastry burns quickly and can result in a slightly bitter taste.*

Because many sweet tarts and tartlets are served cold, always bake the pastry cases blind so that the filling doesn't make the pastry go soggy. For special occasions it's worth making the cases and filling separately in advance and only combining the two at the last possible minute. The sweet crunchiness of the pastry combined with a smooth, creamy filling will more than repay the extra trouble.

Creamy orange tart
The filling uses the rind from three oranges but the juice from only one. Oranges deteriorate as soon as the rind has been removed, so use the remaining oranges as soon as possible.

PREPARATION TIME: 30 minutes, plus chilling

COOKING TIME: 50–55 minutes

OVEN TEMPERATURE: 200°C (400°F), Gas Mark 6, then 160°C (325°F), Gas Mark 3

SERVES 6

175 g (6 oz) pâte sucrée

2 eggs, plus 2 egg yolks

150 g (5 oz) caster sugar

150 ml (¼ pint) single cream

3 oranges

To decorate:

1 orange

75 g (3 oz) caster sugar

3 tablespoons water

150 ml (¼ pint) double cream

1 Make the pastry (*see page 16*). Roll it out and line a deep 20 cm (8 inch) tart tin. Chill the pastry case for 30 minutes and bake blind in a preheated oven for 15 minutes. Remove the paper and beans or foil and return to the oven for a further 5 minutes.

2 Make the filling. Whisk the eggs, egg yolks and sugar in a bowl until foamy. Whisk in the cream. Grate the rind from the oranges and squeeze the juice from one of them. Add the rind and juice to the egg mixture and whisk again. Pour into the pastry case and bake in a preheated oven, 160°C (325°F), Gas Mark 3, for 30–35 minutes or until the filling is firm.

3 Prepare the decoration. Pare the rind from the orange and cut it into thin strips. Put the sugar in a pan with the water and bring to the boil, stirring until the sugar has dissolved. Add the orange rind and boil for 2–3 minutes without stirring until syrupy.

4 Use a slotted spoon to transfer the orange rind from the syrup to a plate. Whip the double cream in a bowl until stiff and decorate the tart. Sprinkle with the glazed orange rind and serve cold.

Lemon tart

Adding lemon rind and juice to the pastry provides the necessary sharpness to complement the creamy sweetness of the filling. This tart is equally good hot or cold.

PREPARATION TIME: 30 minutes, plus chilling and cooling

COOKING TIME: 45 minutes

OVEN TEMPERATURE: 190°C (375°F), Gas Mark 5, then 160°C (325°F), Gas Mark 3

SERVES 6

Pastry:

150 g (5 oz) plain flour

¼ teaspoon baking powder

pinch of salt

65 g (2½ oz) caster sugar

juice and finely grated rind of 3 lemons

125 g (4 oz) chilled butter, diced

1 egg yolk

Filling:

2 eggs

2 egg yolks

50 g (2 oz) caster sugar

4 teaspoons cornflour

finely grated rind of 1 lemon

300 ml (½ pint) milk

300 ml (½ pint) double cream

To decorate:

lemon slices

icing sugar

1 Sift the flour, baking powder and salt on to a cold surface and stir in the sugar and lemon rind. Make a well in the centre for the butter and egg yolk. Work the flour into the butter and egg yolk with your fingertips. Gather the dough, roll it and line a 23 cm (9 inch) loose-based, fluted tart tin. Chill for 30 minutes, then bake blind in a preheated oven for 15 minutes.

2 Meanwhile, whisk the eggs, egg yolks, sugar, cornflour, and lemon rind. Heat the milk, cream and juice in a heavy pan until just below boiling point, then beat into the egg mixture. Return the mixture to the pan and cook over a low heat until thickened, stirring constantly.

3 Pour the custard into the pastry case and bake in a preheated oven, 160°C (325°F), Gas Mark 3, for 30 minutes or until the filling is just set.

4 Leave the tart in the tin until it is lukewarm, then transfer it to a serving dish. Decorate with browned lemon slices and sprinkle with icing sugar.

Plum & lemon tart

The sweet, juicy plums and sharp, fresh lemon custard make a delicious combination in this recipe. Serve the tart warm or cold with lightly whipped cream.

PREPARATION TIME: 30 minutes, plus chilling

COOKING TIME: 40–45 minutes

OVEN TEMPERATURE: 190°C (375°F), Gas Mark 5

SERVES 6–8

175 g (6 oz) rich shortcrust pastry

50 g (2 oz) butter, at room temperature

50 g (2 oz) caster sugar

50 g (2 oz) semolina

grated rind of 1 lemon

1 egg, beaten

750 g (1½ lb) ripe plums, halved and stoned

4 tablespoons apricot jam

whipped cream, to serve

1 Make the pastry (*see page* 15). Roll out the pastry and line a 23 cm (9 inch) tart tin. Prick the pastry base with a fork, then chill for 30 minutes.

2 Make the filling. Beat together the butter and sugar in a bowl until light and fluffy. Beat in the semolina, lemon rind and egg, then spread the mixture over the pastry base. Arrange the plum halves over the top, cut sides down.

3 Bake the tart in a preheated oven for 40–45 minutes until the pastry is browned and the filling golden and set.

4 Warm the jam in a small saucepan, then press it through a sieve into a bowl or jug. Brush the apricot glaze over the tart and serve the cream separately.

Mincemeat & clementine pie
Instead of Christmas pudding, try this light and tasty tart with its orange-flavoured pastry. The juicy clementine segments keep the mincemeat moist and delicious.

PREPARATION TIME: 20 minutes, plus chilling

COOKING TIME: 25–30 minutes

OVEN TEMPERATURE: 200°C (400°F), Gas Mark 6

SERVES 6

Pastry:

75 g (3 oz) plain flour

75 g (3 oz) wholemeal flour

75 g (3 oz) chilled butter, diced

50 g (2 oz) ground almonds

25 g (1 oz) caster sugar

grated rind of 1 orange

1 egg, beaten

Filling:

375 g (12 oz) luxury mincemeat

3 clementines, peeled and segmented

icing sugar, for dusting

1 Make the pastry. Sift the plain and wholemeal flours into a bowl, add the butter and rub in with the fingertips until the mixture resembles fine breadcrumbs. Stir in the ground almonds, sugar and orange rind. Add the egg and mix to a firm dough. Knead the dough briefly on a lightly floured surface, then chill for 30 minutes. Roll out the pastry and line a 20 cm (8 inch) tart tin.

2 Gather up the pastry trimmings, reroll them and cut into holly-leaf shapes. Stick some of the leaves to the edge of the pastry case with a little water and reserve about six. Chill the pastry case for 30 minutes.

3 Mix the mincemeat with the clementine segments in a bowl. Spread the mixture over the pastry case and arrange the reserved holly-leaf shapes over the top.

4 Bake the tart in a preheated oven for 25–30 minutes until the pastry is golden brown. Dust with icing sugar and serve warm or cold.

Apple & orange sponge tart

The addition of self-raising flour to the filling makes a light and spongy filling, which rises around the apple slices.

PREPARATION TIME: 20 minutes, plus chilling

COOKING TIME: 35–40 minutes

OVEN TEMPERATURE: 190°C (375°F), Gas Mark 5

SERVES 6–8

200 g (7 oz) rich shortcrust pastry

125 g (4 oz) butter, softened

125 g (4 oz) caster sugar

2 eggs

125 g (4 oz) self-raising flour

grated rind and juice of 1 orange

3 small eating apples

2 tablespoons apricot jam

1 Make the pastry (*see page* 15). Roll it out and line a deep 23 cm (9 inch) tart tin. Chill the pastry case for 30 minutes.

2 Make the filling. Combine the butter, sugar, eggs, flour and orange rind and juice in a bowl. Beat together for 2–3 minutes until the mixture is light and fluffy and spread it over the pastry case.

3 Peel, quarter and core the apples. Slice each quarter thinly and fan out the slices slightly. Set one in the centre of the filling and space the rest evenly around the edge.

4 Bake the tart in a preheated oven for 35–40 minutes until the pastry is golden and the filling set. Warm the jam in a saucepan, press it through a sieve into a bowl, then brush it over the top of the tart. Serve warm or cold.

Lemon meringue pie

For best results, whisk the egg whites in a clean, dry and grease-free bowl. Some cooks like to add a pinch of salt or a few drops of lemon juice to help the foam keep its shape.

PREPARATION TIME: 35 minutes, plus chilling

COOKING TIME: 50 minutes

OVEN TEMPERATURE: 200°C (400°F), Gas Mark 6

SERVES 6

175 g (6 oz) pâte sucrée

25 g (1 oz) cornflour

100 g (3½ oz) caster sugar

150 ml (¼ pint) water

grated rind of 2 lemons

juice of 1 lemon

25 g butter

2 egg yolks

Meringue:

3 egg whites

175 g (6 oz) caster sugar

1 Make the pastry (*see page* 16). Roll it out and line a 20 cm (8 inch) tart tin. Chill for 30 minutes, then bake blind in a preheated oven for 15 minutes. Remove the paper and beans or foil and return to the oven for a further 5 minutes.

2 Mix the cornflour and caster sugar in a saucepan. Stir in the water, lemon rind and juice until well blended. Bring to the boil, stirring until the sauce is thickened and smooth. Take it off the heat and stir in the butter. Leave to cool slightly.

3 Whisk the egg yolks in a bowl. Whisk in 2 tablespoons of the sauce and return this mixture to the pan. Cook gently until the sauce has thickened further and pour it into the pastry case. Return to the oven for 15 minutes until the filling has set.

4 Whisk the egg whites until stiff and dry. Whisk in 1 tablespoon of sugar, then fold in the rest. Spread the mixture so that it completely covers the filling. Return to the oven for 10 minutes until the meringue is golden. Serve warm or cold.

French apple flan
For a special occasion, sprinkle a few drops of Calvados (the brandy made from distilled cider) over the apple slices when you arrange them in the tart.

PREPARATION TIME: 30 minutes, plus chilling

COOKING TIME: 40–45 minutes

OVEN TEMPERATURE: 220°C (425°F), Gas Mark 7, then 190°C (375°F), Gas Mark 5

SERVES 8

250 g (8 oz) pâte sucrée

750 g (1½ lb) eating apples

3 tablespoons lemon juice

4 tablespoons warmed, sieved apricot jam

175 ml (6 fl oz) single cream

2 eggs, beaten

50 g (2 oz) caster sugar

1 Make the pastry (*see page* 16). Roll it out and line a 25 cm (10 inch) tart tin. Chill the pastry case for 30 minutes.

2 Peel and core the apples. Slice them thinly into a bowl and toss with the lemon juice. Drain the apples and arrange them in concentric circles over the base of the pastry case.

3 Brush the apricot jam over the apple slices and bake the tart in a preheated oven for 10 minutes.

4 Whisk the cream, eggs and sugar in a bowl. Pour the mixture carefully over the apples. Return the flan to the preheated oven and bake at 190°C (375°F), Gas Mark 5, for 30–35 minutes until the pastry is golden and the filling cooked. Serve warm.

French apple flan

Apricot tart

Crème pâtissière can be used in all sorts of fruit tarts. When you leave it to cool, always cover the surface with a piece of damp greaseproof paper to stop a skin forming.

PREPARATION TIME: 20 minutes, plus chilling

COOKING TIME: 50 minutes

OVEN TEMPERATURE: 200°C (400°F), Gas Mark 6, then 190°C (375°F), Gas Mark 5

SERVES 6

175 g (6 oz) pâte sucrée

8 large fresh apricots, halved; reserve 4 stones

150 g (5 oz) vanilla sugar

225 ml (7 fl oz) water

Crème pâtissière:

50 g (2 oz) caster sugar

3 egg yolks

2 tablespoons cornflour

300 ml (½ pint) milk

2–4 drops vanilla essence

1 Make the pâte sucrée (*see page* 16). Roll it out and line a 20 cm (8 inch) loose-based tart tin. Chill the pâte sucrée for 30 minutes, then bake blind in a preheated oven for 15 minutes. Remove the paper and beans or foil, reduce the oven temperature and bake for a further 10 minutes. Remove the pastry case from the tin and leave it to cool.

2 Crack four of the apricot stones and remove the kernels. Put the kernels, sugar and water in a pan and simmer for 5 minutes.

3 Add the apricots and poach for about 10 minutes until the fruit is tender. Drain on kitchen paper.

4 Make the crème pâtissière. Mix together the sugar, egg yolks and cornflour. Heat the milk in a saucepan just to boiling point, then whisk into the egg mixture. Return the mixture to the pan and slowly bring to the boil. Cover the surface with damp greaseproof paper and leave to cool. Spread the crème pâtissière in the pastry case and arrange the fruit on top. Chill until required.

Rhubarb & ginger pie
Use young, brightly coloured stalks of rhubarb, but don't forget to add sugar. No matter how appealing the colour and tender the flesh, rhubarb is always sour.

PREPARATION TIME: 20 minutes, plus chilling

COOKING TIME: 35–40 minutes

OVEN TEMPERATURE: 190°C (375°F), Gas Mark 5

SERVES 6

Pastry:

375 g (12 oz) plain flour

175 g (6 oz) chilled butter, diced

50 g (2 oz) caster sugar

2 teaspoons grated orange rind

1 egg, beaten

2–3 tablespoons iced water

Filling:

750 g (1½ lb) rhubarb, sliced

50 g (2 oz) caster sugar

3 tablespoons orange juice

2 teaspoons ground ginger

50 ml (2 fl oz) double cream

1 Sift the flour into a bowl, add the butter and rub in with the fingertips until the mixture resembles fine breadcrumbs. Stir in the sugar and orange rind, then add the egg and enough cold water to mix to a firm dough. Knead the pastry briefly, then chill for 30 minutes. Roll out just over half the pastry and line a 23 cm (9 inch) pie dish. Bake blind in a preheated oven for 20 minutes. Remove the paper and beans or foil and return to the preheated oven for a further 5 minutes. Set aside to cool.

2 Mix the rhubarb, sugar, orange juice and ginger in a saucepan and simmer for 10–15 minutes. Spread the cream over the base, then spoon on the rhubarb mixture. Serve warm.

Blueberry pie
Fresh blueberries have a fairly short season, but frozen berries are available and can be used equally successfully in this pie. The flavour of this pretty fruit is intensified by cooking.

PREPARATION TIME: 25 minutes, plus chilling

COOKING TIME: 30–35 minutes

OVEN TEMPERATURE: 190°C (375°F), Gas Mark 5

SERVES 6

375 g (12 oz) pâte sucrée

250 g (8 oz) fresh or frozen blueberries, defrosted if frozen

25 g (1 oz) sugar

milk, to glaze

50 g (2 oz) flaked almonds, to decorate

cream or crème fraîche, to serve

1 Make the pastry (*see page* 16). Roll out about two-thirds of it and line a 23 cm (9 inch) tart tin. Chill for 30 minutes. Spread the blueberries evenly over the pastry case and sprinkle with the sugar.

2 Roll out the remaining pastry and cut into thin strips. Brush the rim of the tart with water and arrange the pastry strips in a lattice pattern over the top.

3 Brush the pastry with a little milk and sprinkle the flaked almonds over the surface.

4 Bake in a preheated oven for 30–35 minutes until the pastry is golden and the blueberries are tender. Serve warm or cold with cream or crème fraîche.

Blueberry pie

Raspberry brûlée tart

Make sure that the grill has time to get really hot before you put the finished tart under the heat. The sugar should form a crunchy topping above the smooth, creamy filling.

PREPARATION TIME: 25 minutes, plus chilling

COOKING TIME: 30 minutes

OVEN TEMPERATURE: 200°C (400°F), Gas Mark 6

SERVES 4–6

175 g (6 oz) pâte sucrée

150 ml (¼ pint) double cream

150 ml (¼ pint) thick Greek yogurt

25 g (1 oz) caster sugar

1 teaspoon grated orange rind

125 g (4 oz) raspberries, hulled

50 g (2 oz) golden granulated sugar

1 Make the pastry (*see page* 16). Roll it out and line a deep 20 cm (8 inch) tart tin. Chill the pastry case for 30 minutes, then bake blind in a preheated oven for 15 minutes. Remove the paper and beans or foil and return to the oven for a further 10 minutes.

2 Make the filling. Whip the cream in a bowl until it is stiff, then carefully fold in the yogurt, caster sugar and orange rind.

3 Arrange the raspberries over the base of the pastry case and cover them with the cream mixture. Chill for about 1 hour until the cream mixture is firm.

4 Sprinkle the granulated sugar evenly over the filling, taking care to leave none of the cream mixture exposed. Protect the pastry edges with a strip of foil, then put the tart under a preheated hot grill until the sugar is melted and bubbling. Cool, then chill until ready to serve.

Raspberry & almond tart

Use unsweetened pastry for this tart, which has a rich, sweet filling. The mixture of ground almonds, sugar and eggs is sometimes known as frangipane.

PREPARATION TIME: 25 minutes, plus chilling

COOKING TIME: 35–40 minutes

OVEN TEMPERATURE: 190°C (375°F), Gas Mark 5

SERVES 6–8

175 g (6 oz) rich shortcrust pastry

3 tablespoons seedless raspberry jam

75 g (3 oz) caster sugar

3 eggs

75 g (3 oz) butter, melted

75 g (3 oz) ground almonds

few drops of almond essence

25 g (1 oz) flaked almonds

50 g (2 oz) icing sugar, sifted

1 Make the pastry (*see page* 15). Roll it out and line a 23 cm (9 inch) tart tin. Chill the pastry case for 30 minutes.

2 Spread the jam over the base of the pastry. In a bowl, whisk the caster sugar with the eggs until light and fluffy. Whisk in the melted butter, then stir in the ground almonds and almond essence.

3 Pour the filling into the pastry case and sprinkle with the flaked almonds. Bake in a preheated oven for 35–40 minutes until the pastry is crisp and the filling set. Leave to cool.

4 In a small bowl blend the icing sugar to a paste with a few drops of water, then drizzle it over the tart.

Linzertorte

This delicious tart takes its name from the Austrian town of Linz. It is distinguished by the pastry, which is made with ground almonds.

PREPARATION TIME: 25 minutes

COOKING TIME: 25–30 minutes

OVEN TEMPERATURE: 190°C (375°F) Gas Mark 5

SERVES 6

150 g (6 oz) plain flour

½ teaspoon ground cinnamon

75 g (3 oz) butter

50 g (2 oz) sugar

50 g (2 oz) ground almonds

2 teaspoons finely grated lemon rind

2 large egg yolks

about 1 tablespoon lemon juice

325 g (11 oz) raspberry jam

icing sugar, to decorate

1 Sift the flour and cinnamon into a bowl. Rub in the butter until the mixture resembles fine breadcrumbs. Add the sugar, almonds and lemon rind. Bind the dough with the egg yolks and enough lemon juice to make a stiff dough. Turn out the dough on to a floured surface and knead lightly.

2 Roll out two-thirds of the dough and line a greased 18–20 cm (7–8 inch) fluted flan ring placed on a baking sheet. Make sure the dough is evenly rolled out, press it to the shape of the ring and trim off the excess.

3 Fill the tart with the raspberry jam. Roll out the reserved dough and the trimmings and cut into long strips with a pastry wheel or knife. Use these to make a lattice over the jam.

4 Bake the tart in a preheated oven for 25–30 minutes until golden-brown. Leave to cool, then remove the flan ring. Sprinkle icing sugar over the top just before serving.

Linzertorte

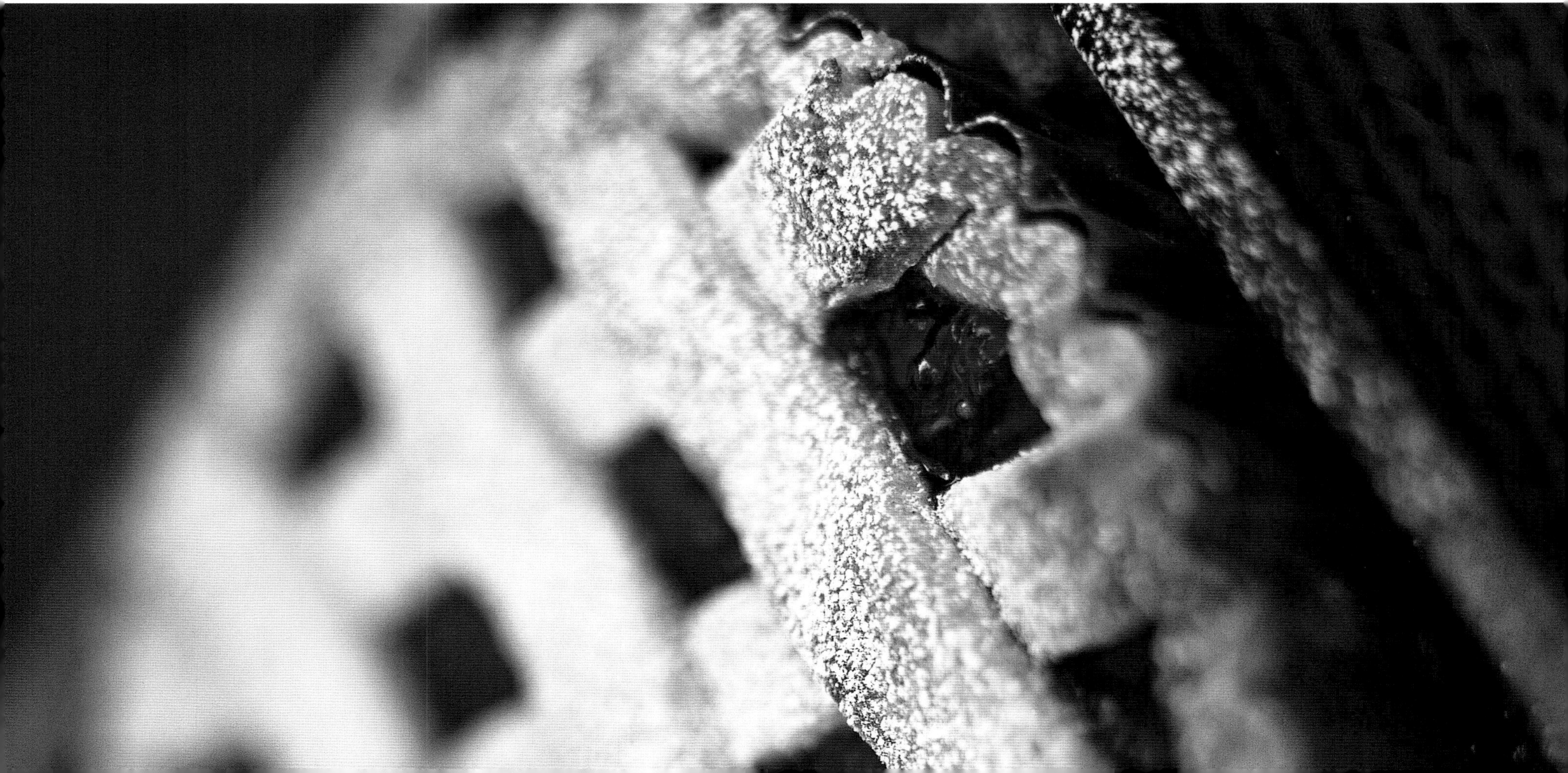

Treacle tart

This old nursery stand-by is hard to beat on a cold winter's day, or indeed on any other day. Serve it with plenty of custard or whipped cream.

PREPARATION TIME: 20 minutes, plus chilling
COOKING TIME: 30–35 minutes
OVEN TEMPERATURE: 190°C (375°F), Gas Mark 5
SERVES 6

250 g (8 oz) shortcrust pastry
275 g (9 oz) golden syrup
175 g (6 oz) fresh white breadcrumbs
grated rind and juice of 2 lemons

1 Make the pastry (*see page* 14). Roll it out and line a deep 20 cm (8 inch) tart tin. Trim the edges.

2 Warm the golden syrup in a saucepan until it is runny, then remove the pan from the heat and stir in the breadcrumbs, lemon rind and juice. Spread the mixture over the pastry case.

3 Bake the tart in a preheated oven for 30–35 minutes until the pastry is crisp and the filling golden. Serve warm or cold, drizzled with extra golden syrup.

Butterscotch meringue pie
Use dark brown muscovado sugar for the rich, creamy filling to create a striking contrast with the white meringue that tops it.

PREPARATION TIME: 35 minutes, plus chilling

COOKING TIME: 35 minutes

OVEN TEMPERATURE: 200°C (400°F), Gas Mark 6

SERVES 6

Pastry:

125 g (4 oz) plain flour

75 g (3 oz) chilled butter, diced

25 g (1 oz) caster sugar

50 g (2 oz) ground hazelnuts

1 egg yolk

2–3 tablespoons iced water

Filling:

50 g (2 oz) cornflour

125 g (4 oz) dark muscovado sugar

300 ml (½ pint) milk

50 g (2 oz) butter, diced

3 egg yolks

1 teaspoon vanilla essence

Meringue:

3 egg whites

175 g (6 oz) caster sugar

1 Make the pastry. Put the flour in a bowl, add the butter and rub in with your fingertips until the mixture resembles breadcrumbs. Stir in the sugar and ground hazelnuts and add the egg yolk and enough water to mix to a firm dough.

2 Knead the dough briefly, roll it out and line a 20 cm (8 inch) tart tin. Chill for 30 minutes, then bake blind in a preheated oven for 15 minutes. Remove the paper and beans or foil and return to the oven for a further 5 minutes.

3 Combine the cornflour and sugar in a saucepan. Blend in the milk until smooth. Heat gently, stirring until thickened, then cook for 1 minute more. Cool the sauce slightly. Beat in the butter, a few pieces at a time, then stir in the egg yolks and vanilla. Pour the filling into the pastry case.

4 Whisk the egg whites until they are stiff and dry. Whisk in 1 tablespoon of the sugar, then fold in the remainder. Spread the meringue over the filling to enclose it completely. Return the pie to the oven for 10 minutes until the meringue is golden. Serve warm or cold.

Baked custard tart
Fresh nutmeg has a far superior flavour to the ready grated spice. Keep nutmegs in an airtight container so that the aroma and flavour are not dissipated.

PREPARATION TIME: 20 minutes plus chilling

COOKING TIME: about 1 hour 10 minutes

OVEN TEMPERATURE: 200°C (400°F), Gas Mark 6, then 160°C (325°F), Gas Mark 3

SERVES 6

175 g (6 oz) shortcrust pastry

4 eggs

25 g (1 oz) caster sugar

½ teaspoon vanilla essence

450 ml (¾ pint) milk

grated nutmeg

1 Make the pastry (*see page 14*). Roll it out and line a 20 cm (8 inch) tart tin. Chill for 30 minutes, then bake blind in a preheated oven for 15 minutes. Remove the paper and beans or foil and return to the oven for a further 5 minutes.

2 Lightly whisk the eggs with the sugar and vanilla essence in a bowl. Heat the milk until warm and whisk into the beaten egg mixture.

3 Strain the custard into the pastry case and sprinkle with grated nutmeg.

4 Bake in a preheated oven, 160°C (325°F), Gas Mark 3, for 45–50 minutes until the custard is set and lightly browned. Serve warm or cold.

Royal curd tart
This is a rich, filling tart, so use unsweetened pastry for the case. Curd cheese gives the filling a creamy smoothness that is not over sweet. Fresh strawberries are a good accompaniment.

PREPARATION TIME: 20 minutes, plus chilling

COOKING TIME: 50–55 minutes

OVEN TEMPERATURE: 200°C (400°F), Gas Mark 6, then 180°C (350°F), Gas Mark 4

SERVES 6

250 g (8 oz) shortcrust pastry

227 g (8 oz) medium-fat curd cheese

50 g (2 oz) ground almonds

50 g (2 oz) caster sugar

2 eggs, separated

grated rind and juice of 1 lemon

50 g (2 oz) sultanas

150 ml (¼ pint) double cream

icing sugar, to decorate

1 Make the pastry (*see page* 14). Roll out the pastry and use it to line a 23 cm (9 inch) flan ring placed on a baking sheet. Prick the base, then chill for 30 minutes.

2 Put the curd cheese into a bowl and blend in the ground almonds, caster sugar and egg yolks. Add the lemon rind and juice, sultanas and cream and mix.

3 Whisk the egg whites until stiff and fold them into the mixture. Pour the mixture into the pastry case and bake in a preheated oven for 20 minutes. Lower the temperature to 180°C (350°F), Gas Mark 4 and cook for a further 30–35 minutes until firm and golden.

4 Dust the tart with icing sugar and serve warm or chilled.

Pumpkin pie
To make pumpkin purée, steam or boil pumpkin chunks for 15–20 minutes until tender, then drain thoroughly. Purée the pieces in a food processor or blender or press them through a sieve.

PREPARATION TIME: 25 minutes

COOKING TIME: 45–50 minutes

OVEN TEMPERATURE: 190°C (375°F), Gas Mark 5

SERVES 6–8

250 g (8 oz) pâte sucrée

250 g (8 oz) pumpkin purée or 475 g (15 oz) can pumpkin purée

2 eggs, beaten

150 ml (¼ pint) single cream

75 g (3 oz) caster sugar

1 teaspoon ground cinnamon

½ teaspoon ground ginger

¼ teaspoon grated nutmeg

To decorate:

150 ml (¼ pint) whipping cream

ground cinnamon

1 Make the pastry (*see page* 16). Roll it out and line a 23 cm (9 inch) pie dish. Gather up the trimmings, reroll them thinly and cut into leaf shapes. Brush the edge of the pie lightly with water and attach the leaves.

2 Make the filling. Mix the pumpkin purée, eggs, cream, sugar and spices in a bowl. Pour into the pastry case.

3 Bake the pie in a preheated oven for 45–50 minutes until the filling has set. Leave to cool.

4 Whip the cream in a bowl until stiff. Spoon cream swirls around the rim of the pie and sprinkle with a little ground cinnamon.

Rocky road tart

If you want to freeze this tart in advance, cover it closely with clingfilm and foil once the topping has frozen. Put it in the refrigerator for 30 minutes before serving to soften the topping.

PREPARATION TIME: 15 minutes, plus chilling

COOKING TIME: none

SERVES 8

Base:

300 g (10 oz) ginger or digestive biscuits

125 g (4 oz) butter, melted

50 ml (2 oz) honey

Filling:

150 g (5 oz) honey and almond chocolate

1 tablespoon melted butter

75 ml (3 fl oz) double cream

450 ml (¾ pint) chocolate ice cream

450 ml (¾ pint) strawberry ice cream

450 ml (¾ pint) vanilla ice cream

100 g (3½ oz) mini-marshmallows

50 g (2 oz) pecan nuts, roughly chopped

fresh cherries or strawberries, to decorate (optional)

1 Put the biscuits in a plastic bag and tap them with a rolling pin to make crumbs. Mix the butter, honey and biscuit crumbs together in a bowl. Spoon the mixture into a 25 cm (10 inch) tart tin, pressing it down into the base and up the sides with the back of a spoon. Chill for 30 minutes.

2 Put the chocolate, butter and cream into a heatproof bowl above a pan of simmering water until the mixture is melted and smooth. Leave to one side to cool.

3 Scoop the ice creams on to the biscuit base, alternating the flavours as you go. Sprinkle the top with the marshmallows and pecan nuts. Drizzle the tart with the chocolate sauce and freezer it for 2 hours. Decorate with fresh fruit before serving, if liked.

Chocolate pear slice
This quick dessert is smart enough for a special occasion but not too heavy if rich dishes have preceded it. It can be prepared in advance and cooked just before serving.

PREPARATION TIME: 30 minutes

COOKING TIME: about 30 minutes

OVEN TEMPERATURE: 200°C (400°F), Gas Mark 6, then 230°C (450°F), Gas Mark 8

SERVES 6

2 large ripe pears

2 tablespoons lemon juice

350 g (11½ oz) puff pastry, defrosted if frozen

150 g (5 oz) plain chocolate, broken into pieces

beaten egg, to glaze

icing sugar, for dusting

pouring cream, to serve

1 Quarter, core and thinly slice the pears. Put the pear slices in a bowl of water with the lemon juice.

2 Make the pastry (*see pages* 17–18). Roll it out to a 30 x 18 cm (12 x 7 inch) rectangle and put on a prepared baking sheet. Use the tip of a sharp knife to make a shallow cut around the pastry, about 1 cm (½ inch) in from the edges; do not cut right through the pastry.

3 Melt the chocolate and spread it over the pastry to within 1 cm (½ inch) of the cut line. Drain the pears and arrange the slices over the chocolate, keeping them just inside the cut line. Make small indentations on the edges of the pastry with the back of a knife. Brush the pastry edges with beaten egg and bake in a preheated oven for about 25 minutes until the pastry is risen and golden.

4 Raise the oven temperature to 230°C (450°F), Gas Mark 8. Generously dust the pastry and pears with icing sugar and return the dish to the oven for about 5 minutes until golden brown. Leave to cool slightly, then serve warm with pouring cream.

Chocolate velvet pie
This chocolate shortbread base is an interesting variation on traditional plain shortbread. Swirls of whipped double cream would make a decadent finishing touch.

PREPARATION TIME: 35 minutes plus chilling

COOKING TIME: 22 minutes

OVEN TEMPERATURE: 180°C (350°F), Gas Mark 4

SERVES 10

Shortbread:

175 g (6 oz) plain flour

2 teaspoons cocoa powder

125 g (4 oz) unsalted butter, diced

25 g (1 oz) caster sugar

Filling:

4 teaspoons powdered gelatine

3 tablespoons cold water

125 g (4 oz) caster sugar

3 egg yolks

1 tablespoon cornflour

600 ml (1 pint) milk

2 tablespoons finely ground espresso coffee

50 g (2 oz) plain chocolate, broken into pieces

chocolate shavings, to decorate

1 Rub the butter into the sifted flour and cocoa powder, add the sugar and mix to a dough. Press evenly over the base and sides of a deep 20 cm (8 inch) fluted tart tin. Bake for 20 minutes in a preheated oven, then leave to cool.

2 Soak the gelatine in water. Whisk the sugar, egg yolks, cornflour and 2 tablespoons of milk. Bring the rest of the milk to the boil with the coffee powder. Whisk it into the egg mixture.

3 Return the mixture to the saucepan and heat gently, stirring until it thickens. Remove from the heat and beat in the gelatine until dissolved. Add the chocolate and stir until it has melted. Cool slightly then pour the mixture into the tart case. Chill for several hours.

4 Transfer the pie to a plate and scatter generously with chocolate shavings.

Chocolate velvet pie

Pear, red wine & walnut tart *Serve this rich tart cold.*

When you are slicing the pears, try not to distort their shape so that they are recognizable when they are arranged over the custard.

PREPARATION TIME: 15 minutes, plus chilling

COOKING TIME: 45 minutes

OVEN TEMPERATURE: 200°C (400°F), Gas Mark 6

SERVES 6

Pastry:

175 g (6 oz) plain flour

75 g (3 oz) chilled butter, diced

50 g (2 oz) caster sugar

25 g (1 oz) walnuts, finely chopped

1 egg yolk

1–2 tablespoons iced water

Pears:

4 ripe pears

1 tablespoon lemon juice

300 ml (½ pint) red wine

125 g (4 oz) caster sugar

1 cinnamon stick

4 tablespoons redcurrant jelly

Filling:

150 ml (¼ pint) thick cold custard

150 ml (¼ pint) double cream

1 Sift the flour into a bowl, add the butter and rub in with the fingertips until the mixture resembles breadcrumbs. Stir in the caster sugar and walnuts and add the egg yolk and just enough water to make a firm dough. Roll out the pastry and line a 23 cm (9 inch) tart tin. Chill the pastry case for 30 minutes, then bake blind in a preheated oven for 15 minutes. Remove the paper and beans or foil and return the tart to the oven for a further 10 minutes.

2 Peel, halve and core the pears. Brush them with the lemon juice to prevent discoloration. Combine the wine, sugar and cinnamon stick in a saucepan. Bring to the boil, add the pears and poach gently for about 10 minutes until they are tender but still firm. Use a slotted spoon to remove the pears and cinnamon stick from the syrup. Discard the cinnamon. Boil the syrup for about 10 minutes until it is thick and syrupy and stir in the redcurrant jelly.

3 Brush the inside of the pastry case with a little of the red wine syrup. Whisk the custard in a bowl until it is fluffy. Whip the cream in a separate bowl until stiff, then fold into the custard. Spread the mixture over the pastry case. Slice the pears thinly and arrange them over the filling, then brush with the remaining red wine syrup.

Tarte Tatin
This version of the classic French tart is deceptively simple to make. Use flavourful, crunchy apples, such as Cox's, and unsalted butter.

PREPARATION TIME: 20 minutes, plus chilling

COOKING TIME: 35–40 minutes

OVEN TEMPERATURE: 200°C (400°F), Gas Mark 6

SERVES 4–6

175 g (6 oz) pâte sucrée
50 g (2 oz) butter
50 g (2 oz) caster sugar
6 dessert apples, peeled, cored and quartered
thick cream or crème fraîche, to serve

1 Make the pastry (*see page* 16). Wrap it closely in clingfilm and leave it to chill for 30 minutes.

2 Melt the butter and sugar in a 20 cm (8 inch) ovenproof frying pan. When the mixture is golden brown, add the apples and toss them in the syrup to coat them. Cook for a few minutes until the apples start to caramelize.

3 Roll out the pastry on a lightly floured surface to a round, a little larger than the pan. Put it over the apples, tucking the edges of the pastry inside the edge of the pan until it fits neatly.

4 Bake in a preheated oven for 35–40 minutes until the pastry is golden. Leave to cool in the pan for 5 minutes, then put a large plate on top of the pan and invert the tart on to it. Serve warm with thick cream or crème fraîche.

Lemon & passion fruit pie
In this unusual American pie, the tartness of the lemon tempers the mild sweetness of the yellow-fleshed passion fruit.

PREPARATION TIME: 25 minutes, plus chilling

COOKING TIME: 40–45 minutes

OVEN TEMPERATURE: 200°C (400°F), Gas Mark 6, then 160°C (325°F), Gas Mark 3

SERVES 8

175 g (6 oz) pâte sucrée

4 eggs

50 g (2 oz) sugar

150 ml (¼ pint) double cream

finely grated rind and juice of 3 lemons

To decorate:

seeds from 3 passion fruit

150 ml (¼ pint) double cream, beaten until just holding its shape

1 Make the pastry (*see page* 16). Roll it out and line a 20 cm (8 inch) fluted tart tin. Chill for 30 minutes, then trim the dough. Bake blind in a preheated oven for 15 minutes. Remove the beans and paper or foil and return the pastry case to the oven for a further 5 minutes.

2 Make the filling. Beat together the eggs and sugar, then stir in the cream and lemon rind and juice.

3 Pour the mixture into the pastry case, level the top and bake in a preheated oven, 160°C (325°F), Gas Mark 3, for 25–30 minutes until just set. Leave to cool.

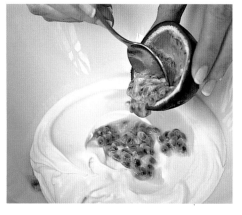

4 Stir the seeds of two of the passion fruit into the cream, then spoon over the pie. Sprinkle with the remaining seeds and serve within 1 hour.

Mascarpone & date tart

The crisp, slightly sweet pastry is a wonderful contrast to the smooth, creamy mascarpone cheese. Fresh dates make an unusual filling.

PREPARATION TIME: 15 minutes, plus chilling

COOKING TIME: about 1 hour

OVEN TEMPERATURE: 180°C (350°F), Gas Mark 4

SERVES 8

200 g (7 oz) pâte sucrée

250 g (8 oz) fresh dates, halved and pitted

250 g (8 oz) mascarpone cheese

125 ml (4 fl oz) double cream

2 eggs, lightly beaten

2 tablespoons caster sugar

1 tablespoon cornflour

2 teaspoons vanilla essence

1 Make the pastry (*see page* 16). Roll out the dough and line a 23 cm (9 inch) fluted tart tin. Ease the pastry into the tin, then chill for 30 minutes.

2 Trim the edges of the pastry case and bake blind in a preheated oven for 10 minutes. Remove the paper and beans or foil and return the pastry case to the oven for a further 10 minutes. Leave to cool.

3 Scatter the dates evenly over the base of the cooked pastry case. Combine the mascarpone, cream, eggs, sugar, cornflour and vanilla essence in a bowl and whisk until smooth.

4 Pour the mixture into the pastry case and bake for 35 minutes, or until the filling is golden and set.

Summer fruit flan
This delicious summer flan filled with luscious berry fruits is perfect for a dinner party. Not only does it look special but it serves up to 10 people.

PREPARATION TIME: 30 minutes, plus chilling

COOKING TIME: 20 minutes

OVEN TEMPERATURE: 220°C (425°F), Gas Mark 7

SERVES 8–10

500 g (1 lb) puff pastry, defrosted if frozen

beaten egg, to glaze

a few whole cherries, to decorate

Custard filling:

1 egg

50 g (2 oz) caster sugar

40 g (1½ oz) plain flour

300 ml (½ pint) milk

25 g (1 oz) butter, diced

few drops of vanilla essence

Fruit filling:

250 g (8 oz) strawberries, hulled and sliced

125 g (4 oz) raspberries, hulled

250 g (8 oz) cherries, stoned and halved

3 peaches, sliced

125 g (4 oz) redcurrants, stemmed

125 g (4 oz) blackberries, stemmed

4 tablespoons redcurrant or bramble jelly

1 Make the pastry (*see pages* 17–18). Roll it out to a 30 cm (12 inch) square. Put it on a baking sheet, trim a 2.5 cm (1 inch) strip from each side and brush the edges with egg. Lay the strips around the edge to form a case, trimming to fit at the corners. Press them down to seal, and pinch the edges.

2 Prick the base with a fork, brush the edges with egg and bake in a preheated oven for 20 minutes until the pastry is risen and golden brown. Cool on a wire rack.

3 Whisk the egg and sugar in a bowl until frothy, then whisk in the flour and 1 tablespoon of milk. Heat the rest of the milk and pour it in. Return the mixture to the pan and cook over a moderate heat, stirring until it is thick and smooth. Off the heat, beat in the butter and vanilla. Cover closely and leave to cool.

4 Spread the custard over the pastry case and arrange the fruit on top. Decorate with the cherries. Warm the jelly and brush over the fruit and pastry edges. Chill for 2 hours.

Cheesecake tart with Grand Marnier berries

Soaking the dried berries in the liqueur not only plumps them up but also ensures that the orange flavour permeates the filling.

PREPARATION TIME: 15 minutes, plus chilling

COOKING TIME: about 1 hour

OVEN TEMPERATURE: 180°C (350°F), Gas Mark 4

SERVES 8

175 g (6 oz) dried mixed berries and cherries

5 tablespoons Grand Marnier

2 tablespoons clear honey

grated rind of 1 lemon

200 g (7 oz) rich shortcrust pastry

250 g (8 oz) ricotta cheese

200 g (7 oz) cream cheese

100 g (3½ oz) caster sugar

3 whole eggs, plus 1 yolk

25 g (1 oz) flaked almonds

1 Put the dried fruit in a small pan with the Grand Marnier, honey and lemon rind. Warm over a low heat until the liquid starts to boil. Remove from the heat, cover and leave until cold.

2 Make the pastry (*see page* 15). Roll it out and line a 23 cm (9 inch) tart tin. Leave to chill for 30 minutes, then trim away the excess pastry. Bake blind in a preheated oven for 20 minutes. Remove the paper and beans or foil and return the tart to the oven for a further 5 minutes.

3 Beat together the two cheeses, sugar and eggs to make a smooth custard. Stir in half of the dried fruit mixture and pour into the pastry case. Bake for 35 minutes until the tart is firm to the touch and golden on top.

4 Spoon the remaining dried fruit mixture over the top and top with the flaked almonds. Leave to cool and serve with a glass of Grand Marnier.

Chocolate, maple & pecan tart

This superb tart is similar to a classic pecan pie, but with the addition of a chocolate filling. It's good served warm or chilled.

PREPARATION TIME: 30 minutes, plus chilling

COOKING TIME: 35–40 minutes

OVEN TEMPERATURE: 180°C (350°F), Gas Mark 4, then 230°C (450°F), Gas Mark 8

SERVES 8

200 g (7 oz) plain chocolate, broken into pieces

50 g (2 oz) unsalted butter

75 g (3 oz) caster sugar

175 ml (6 fl oz) maple syrup

3 eggs

350 g (11½ oz) pâte sucrée or puff pastry, defrosted if frozen

125 g (4 oz) pecan nuts

icing sugar, for dusting

1 Melt the chocolate in a bowl over simmering water, then stir in the butter. Put the sugar and maple syrup in a saucepan and heat gently until the sugar dissolves. Leave to cool slightly. Lightly whisk the eggs to a smooth consistency. Whisk in the chocolate and syrup mixtures.

2 Make the pastry (*see pages* 16 or 17–18). Roll it out and line a deep 23 cm (9 inch) tart tin. Chill for 30 minutes. Pour the filling into the pastry case. Put it on a warm baking sheet and cook in a preheated oven for 15 minutes until the filling is just beginning to set.

3 Remove the tart from the oven and scatter the pecan nuts over the top. Bake for a further 10 minutes until the nuts are just beginning to brown. Increase the oven temperature to 230°C (450°F), Gas Mark 8.

4 Dust the tart generously with icing sugar and return to the oven for about 5 minutes until the nuts are beginning to caramelize. Leave to cool for 20 minutes before serving.

Chocolate swirl tart

This tart is so easy to make that it will quickly become a firm favourite. The amaretti biscuits add a delicious almond flavour.

PREPARATION TIME: 20 minutes, plus chilling

COOKING TIME: none

SERVES 6–8

Crumb shell:

125 g (4 oz) digestive biscuits

50 g (2 oz) amaretti biscuits

6 tablespoons butter

Filling:

200 g (7 oz) plain chocolate

250 ml (8 fl oz) double cream

1 Put the biscuits in a plastic bag and crush them with a rolling pin. Melt the butter in a saucepan and stir in the biscuit crumbs. Press the mixture into a greased 23 cm (9 inch) pie dish. Chill until firm.

2 Put the chocolate in a heatproof bowl over a pan of hot water. Stir gently until melted. Cover a rolling pin with foil and brush lightly with oil. Drizzle a little chocolate on to the rolling pin in zigzag lines, about 2.5 cm (1 inch) long. Chill until set.

3 Beat the cream until stiff and fold into the remaining melted chocolate. Spoon into the crumb case and chill for 2 hours until set.

4 Just before serving, carefully peel the chocolate decorations from the foil and arrange them in the centre of the tart.

White chocolate & almond tart with mint

cream *Mint and chocolate are the perfect combination of flavours, refreshing and sweet, the one enhancing the other.*

PREPARATION TIME: 15 minutes, plus chilling

COOKING TIME: 40 minutes

OVEN TEMPERATURE: 180°C (350°F), Gas Mark 4

SERVES 6–8

300 g (10 oz) pâte sucrée

125 g (4 oz) ground almonds

50 g (2 oz) caster sugar

125 g (4 oz) butter

2 large eggs

200 g (7 oz) white chocolate, finely chopped

25 g (1 oz) flaked almonds

25 g (1 oz) white chocolate, grated, to decorate

Mint cream:

300 ml (½ pint) double cream

2 tablespoons chopped mint

2 tablespoons caster sugar

1 Make the pastry (*see page* 16). Roll it out and line a 23 cm (9 inch) fluted tart tin. Chill for 30 minutes.

2 Put the almonds, sugar, butter and eggs in a food processor. Blitz until smooth. Add the white chocolate and pulse a few times to mix the chocolate through the mixture.

3 Spoon the chocolate mixture into the prepared tart case, sprinkle with flaked almonds and bake in a preheated oven for 40 minutes until the filling is golden and set on top.

4 Remove the tart from the oven and sprinkle with the grated white chocolate. Whisk together the cream, mint and sugar until thick and serve with the warm tart.

White chocolate cherry tart

The perfect marriage of chocolate and cherries is both traditional and highly successful. Cinnamon and chocolate is another favourite partnership.

PREPARATION TIME: 30 minutes, plus chilling

COOKING TIME: about 1 hour

OVEN TEMPERATURE: 200°C (400°F), Gas Mark 6, then 180°C (350°F), Gas Mark 4

SERVES 6–8

Pastry:

175 g (6 oz) plain flour

½ teaspoon ground cinnamon

125 g (4 oz) unsalted butter, diced

25 g (1 oz) caster sugar

2–3 tablespoons iced water

Filling:

2 eggs

40 g (1½ oz) caster sugar

150 g (5 oz) white chocolate, finely chopped

300 ml (½ pint) double cream

450 g (1 lb) fresh black or red cherries, stoned, or 2 x 425 g (14 oz) cans stoned black or red cherries, drained

ground cinnamon, for dusting

1 Make the pastry. Sift the flour and cinnamon into a bowl, add the butter and rub in with the fingertips. Add the sugar and just enough water to mix to a firm dough. Roll out the dough and line a 23 cm (9 inch) loose-based tart tin. Chill for 30 minutes, then bake blind in a preheated oven for 10 minutes. Remove the paper and beans or foil and return to the oven for a further 5 minutes.

2 Beat together the eggs and sugar. Heat the chocolate and cream in a small bowl over hot water until the chocolate has melted. Pour over the egg mixture, stirring constantly.

3 Arrange the cherries in the flan case. Pour the chocolate mixture over the cherries.

4 Bake in the preheated oven, 180°C (350°F), Gas Mark 4, for about 45 minutes until the chocolate cream is set. Dust with cinnamon and serve warm.

Espresso tart with chocolate pastry *This rich, indulgent tart is surprisingly simple to make. For an extra treat, you can decorate the top with chocolate coffee beans.*

PREPARATION TIME: 15 minutes, plus chilling

COOKING TIME: 1 hour

OVEN TEMPERATURE: 180°C (350°F), Gas Mark 4

SERVES 8

Pastry:

200 g (7 oz) flour

35 g (1½ oz) good quality cocoa powder

50 g (2 oz) golden caster sugar

150 g (5 oz) butter, diced

1 large egg, beaten

2–3 tablespoons iced water

Filling:

450 ml (¾ pint) double cream

3 eggs

125 g (4 oz) golden caster sugar

2 tablespoons instant espresso coffee powder

25 g (1 oz) dark chocolate, grated

1 Make the pastry. Sift the flour and cocoa powder into a bowl. Add the sugar and butter and mix with the fingertips until the mixture resembles breadcrumbs. Add the egg and just enough water to make a firm dough. Roll out the pastry and line a 23 cm (9 inch) tart tin. Chill for 30 minutes, then trim the edges.

2 Bake the pastry case blind in a preheated oven for 15 minutes. Remove the beans and paper or foil and return the tart to the oven for a further 10 minutes.

3 Heat the cream until it boils. Whisk the eggs, sugar and coffee powder then pour the hot cream over them, stirring continually. Pour the mixture through a fine sieve and then into the tart case.

4 Bake for 30–35 minutes or until set. Remove from the oven and sprinkle with grated dark chocolate. Leave to cool before serving.

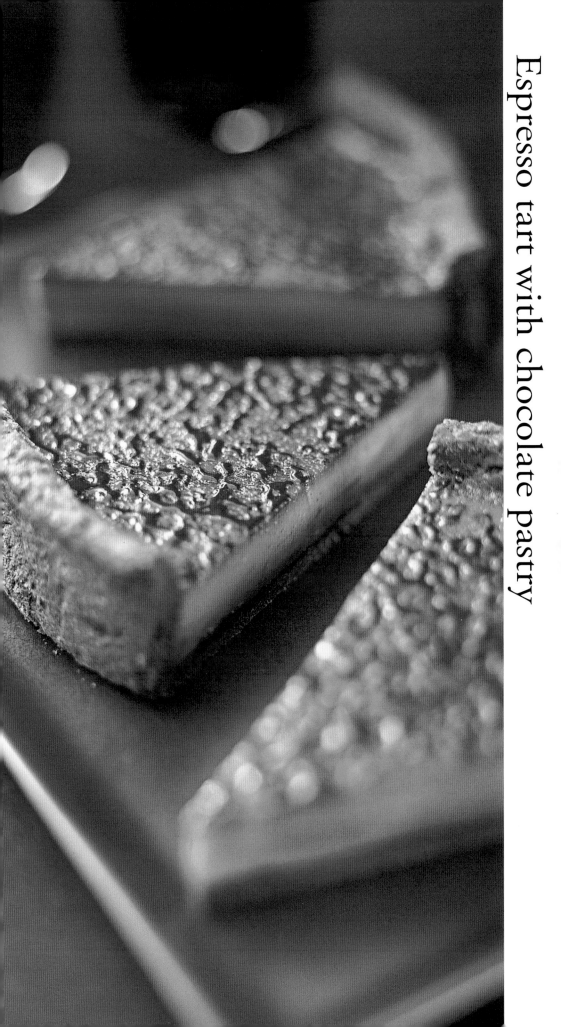

Espresso tart with chocolate pastry

Praline choux tart

Choux pastry doesn't take long to make, but the results always look spectacular. Make this tart for a special occasion. Fresh ripe strawberries are the finishing touch.

PREPARATION TIME: 30 minutes

COOKING TIME: 30 minutes

OVEN TEMPERATURE: 200°C (400°F), Gas Mark 6

SERVES 6

75 g (3 oz) choux pastry

150 g (5 oz) whole almonds, lightly toasted and roughly chopped

150 g (5 oz) caster sugar

175 ml (6 oz) mascarpone cheese

50 ml (2 fl oz) double cream

1 tablespoon icing sugar

3 tablespoons water

fresh berries, to decorate (optional)

1 Make the pastry (*see page* 19). Spoon just over one-third of the mixture on to a baking sheet and use the back of a spoon to spread it out into a 22 cm (8½ inch) disc. Space small spoonfuls of the remaining mixture well apart on another baking sheet. Bake in a preheated oven for 20 minutes until golden.

2 Pierce each bun once and the base a few times for the steam to escape. Return to the oven for 5 minutes to dry. If the base is not dry enough give it 5 minutes more. Cool the pastry on a wire rack.

3 Put the almonds on a lightly greased foil. Melt the sugar with the water over medium heat until a rich golden colour. Pour over the almonds and leave to cool. Break the praline into pieces. Crush half in a plastic bag with a rolling pin.

4 Whisk the mascarpone, cream and crushed praline until thickened. Attach the buns around the sides of the pastry base with a little cream. Spoon the rest into the centre of the tart. Dust with icing sugar and decorate the tart with the remaining praline pieces and fresh berries.

Mango tartlets with passion fruit cream

When you are buying mangoes, choose well-coloured fruit with a shiny, supple skin. Slice downwards, on each side of the large stone.

PREPARATION TIME: 15 minutes

COOKING TIME: 15–20 minutes

OVEN TEMPERATURE: 200°C (400°F), Gas Mark 6

SERVES 4

250 g (8 oz) puff pastry, defrosted if frozen

2 ripe mangoes, peeled, stoned and thinly sliced

25 g (1 oz) butter, melted

100 g (3½ oz) caster sugar

mint sprigs, to decorate

Passion fruit cream:

2–3 passion fruit

125 ml (4 fl oz) single cream

1 Make the pastry (*see pages* 17–18). Roll it out to 5 mm (¼ inch) thick and cut out four 12 cm (5 inch) circles. Put the circles on two prepared baking sheets. Prick the pastry all over with a fork.

2 Arrange the mango slices on the pastry circles. Spoon the melted butter over the mango slices and pastry and sprinkle the sugar over the top.

3 Bake the tarts in a preheated oven for 15–20 minutes or until pastry is cooked and golden.

4 While the tartlets are cooking, cut the passion fruit in half and use a teaspoon to scoop out their pulp into a small bowl. Stir in the cream and mix together thoroughly. Put the tartlets on individual plates and spoon the cream around them. Decorate with mint sprigs and serve immediately.

Strawberry & almond tartlets
The almond-flavoured pastry is delicious with a variety of fillings. Try crushed amaretti biscuits mixed with whipped cream and topped with fruit.

PREPARATION TIME: 30 minutes, plus chilling and setting

COOKING TIME: about 20 minutes

OVEN TEMPERATURE: 190°C (375°F), Gas Mark 5

SERVES 8

Pastry:

250 g (8 oz) butter

125 g (4 oz) caster sugar

2 egg yolks

375 g (12 oz) plain flour, sifted

125 g (4 oz) ground almonds

Filling:

250 g (8 oz) full-fat soft cheese

1 tablespoon caster sugar

1 teaspoon grated lemon rind

750 g (1½ lb) strawberries

5 tablespoons redcurrant jelly, melted

4 tablespoons blanched almonds, toasted

1 Put the butter and sugar in a bowl and cream until light and fluffy. Beat in the egg yolks. Gradually stir in the flour and ground almonds, and knead to a smooth dough. Cover closely and chill for 1 hour.

2 Divide the dough into 8 or 16 pieces. Roll out each one into a round to line eight 11 cm (4½ inch) or 16 smaller tartlet tins. Bake the pastry cases blind in a preheated oven for 15 minutes. Remove the paper and beans or foil and return to the oven for a further 3–4 minutes. Leave to cool in the tins on a wire rack.

3 Make the filling. Beat together the cheese, sugar and lemon rind. Spread a little of the cheese mixture in each pastry case. Reserve 8 or 16 of the best strawberries. Hull and halve the remainder, then put them in the pastry cases.

4 Spoon the redcurrant jelly over the strawberries and leave to set. Just before serving, top with the reserved strawberries and scatter over the toasted almonds.

Cranberry & almond tartlets

If you use frozen cranberries in these tartlets, make sure they are properly defrosted first, although they will lose their shape as they thaw.

PREPARATION TIME: 20 minutes, plus chilling

COOKING TIME: 35–40 minutes

OVEN TEMPERATURE: 190°C (375°F), Gas Mark 5

SERVES 4

175 g (6 oz) pâte sucrée

125 g (4 oz) softened butter

125 g (4 oz) sugar

2 eggs, beaten

125 g (4 oz) ground almonds

few drops of almond essence

2 tablespoons plain flour

3 tablespoons cranberry jelly

75 g (3 oz) cranberries

icing sugar, for dusting

1 Make the pastry (*see page* 16). Divide it into four pieces and roll out each piece to line a 10 cm (4 inch) tartlet tin. Prick each base with a fork and chill while you make the filling.

2 Beat together the butter and sugar until light and fluffy. Add the beaten egg, a little at a time, then add the almonds, almond essence and the flour. Mix well.

3 Spread the cranberry jelly over the tartlet cases. Divide the almond mixture among the pastry cases and smooth the tops. Arrange the cranberries over the top.

4 Bake the tartlets in a preheated oven for 35–40 minutes until the filling is risen and firm. Cool in the tins for 5 minutes, then dust the tops with icing sugar. Serve warm or cold.

Peach & raspberry tartlets

These tempting tartlets are simple to make. The tartlet can be cooked several hours ahead, but should be filled just before eating to prevent the pastry going soft.

PREPARATION TIME: 15 minutes

COOKING TIME: 8–10 minutes

OVEN TEMPERATURE: 190°C (375°F), Gas Mark 5

SERVES 4

15 g (½ oz) butter, melted

4 sheets filo pastry, each about 25 cm (10 inches) square

125 ml (4 fl oz) double cream

1 tablespoon soft brown sugar

2 peaches, peeled, halved, stoned and diced

50 g (2 oz) raspberries

icing sugar, to dust

1 Grease 4 deep muffin tins with the melted butter. Cut a sheet of filo pastry in half, then across into 4 equal-sized squares. Use these filo squares to line each muffin tin, arranging them at slightly different angles. Press them down well, tucking the pastry into the tin neatly. Repeat with the remaining pastry.

2 Bake the filo pastry tartlets in a preheated oven for 8–10 minutes or until golden. Carefully remove the tartlet cases from the tins and leave to cool on a wire rack.

3 Pour the cream into a bowl and add the sugar. Whip lightly until it holds its shape. Spoon the cream into the tartlet cases and top with the peaches and raspberries. Dust with icing sugar. Serve at once.

Baked fig tarts

Figs are an ancient fruit, cultivated by the ancient Egyptians as long ago as 1900 BC. If you prefer, you can use plums instead of figs in this recipe.

PREPARATION TIME: 20 minutes, plus chilling

COOKING TIME: 25–40 minutes

OVEN TEMPERATURE: 200°C (400°F), Gas Mark 6

SERVES 6

400 g (13 oz) pâte sucrée

125 g (4 oz) caster sugar

1 vanilla pod, split

150 ml (¼ pint) orange juice

6 figs

125 g (4 oz) ground almonds

50 g (2 oz) butter

3 medium eggs, beaten

5 tablespoons plum jam

icing sugar, for dusting

thick cream or crème fraîche, to serve

1 Make the pastry (*see page* 16). Roll it out and line a 20 cm (8 inch) loose-based tart tin or four individual 10 cm (4 inch) loose-bottomed tart tins. Chill for 30 minutes, then bake the pastry blind in a preheated oven for 10 minutes. Remove the paper and beans or foil and return to the oven for a further 5 minutes.

2 Cream the butter with 75 g (3 oz) sugar and gradually add the beaten eggs. Beat well and then add the ground almonds. Spread the jam over the bottom of the pastry and then spoon the cake mixture over the top. Arrange the figs on top.

3 Bake for 10–12 minutes for individual tarts or 20 minutes for a large one in a preheated oven or until the sponge has risen and is firm to the touch. Put the remaining sugar in a saucepan with the vanilla pod and orange juice and heat gently to dissolve the sugar, then boil to reduce. Brush over the figs. Leave to cool. Dust with icing sugar and serve with thick cream or crème fraîche.

Banana & mango tartlets
Bananas and mangoes give a tropical flavour to these delicious little tarts, but you could use any combination of your favourite fresh fruits.

PREPARATION TIME: 20 minutes, plus chilling

COOKING TIME: 15 minutes

OVEN TEMPERATURE: 200°C (400°F), Gas Mark 6

SERVES 6

500 g (1 lb) pâte sucrée

6 tablespoons apricot conserve

2 bananas

1 tablespoon lemon juice

1 tablespoon clear honey

1 vanilla pod, split

2 tablespoons double cream

1 small mango

icing sugar, for dusting

mint leaves, to decorate

1 Make the pastry (*see page* 16). Roll it out and line six 12.5 cm (5 inch) tartlet tins. Chill for 15 minutes, then bake the pastry cases blind in a preheated oven for 10 minutes. Remove the paper and beans or foil and return the tartlets to the oven for a further 5 minutes.

2 Spread the apricot conserve over the base of the warm pastry cases. Mash the bananas in a bowl with a fork. Add the lemon juice and stir in the honey to make a smooth, creamy mixture.

3 Scrape the seeds out of the vanilla pod, add them to the banana mixture together with the cream and divide among the pastry cases.

4 Cut the mango flesh off the stone, peel away the skin and slice the flesh. Arrange the slices on top of the banana cream. Dust liberally with icing sugar and serve topped with mint leaves.

Toffee apple pecan tarts
If you cannot find pecan nuts for this recipe, use walnuts, which both look and taste similar to pecans. Granny Smiths are the best apples for the sauce.

PREPARATION TIME: 25 minutes, plus chilling

COOKING TIME: 40–45 minutes

OVEN TEMPERATURE: 200°C (400°F), Gas Mark 6

MAKES 12

250 g (8 oz) pâte sucrée

500 g (1 lb) tart green apples, peeled, cored and chopped

1 tablespoon water

50 g (2 oz) sugar

Filling:

50 g (2 oz) butter

50 g (2 oz) soft brown sugar

1 tablespoon light corn syrup

50 g (2 oz) pecan halves

1 Make the pastry (*see page* 16). Roll it out and cut twelve 8 cm (3 inch) rounds. Line 12 deep tartlet tins with the dough. Chill for 15 minutes, then bake the pastry cases blind in a preheated oven for 15 minutes. Remove the paper and beans or foil and leave to cool.

2 Put the apples in a sauce pan with the water, cover tightly and cook gently for about 5 minutes. Remove the pan from the heat and stir in the sugar. If the apple sauce is too liquid, return it to the heat and simmer for a few more minutes. Leave to cool slightly.

3 Make the filling. Put the butter, soft brown sugar and corn syrup in a saucepan and heat gently, stirring, until the butter has melted, then boil for 2–3 minutes until thickened. Remove from the heat and stir in the nuts.

4 Fill the tartlet cases with apple sauce, then top with a little toffee pecan mixture. Return the tartlets to the oven for 10–15 minutes until bubbling and leave to cool in the tins for 5 minutes.

Lemon curd tartlets

Home-made lemon curd is delicious but doesn't keep well, so use some of it up in these little tarts. Alternatively, use a good quality ready-made curd.

PREPARATION TIME: 20 minutes, plus chilling

COOKING TIME: 20–25 minutes

OVEN TEMPERATURE: 190°C (375°F), Gas Mark 5

MAKES 9

175 g (6 oz) shortcrust pastry
4 tablespoons lemon curd
250 g (8 oz) curd cheese, softened
2 eggs, beaten
50 g (2 oz) caster sugar
grated nutmeg, for sprinkling
icing sugar, for dusting

1 Make the pastry (*see page* 14). Roll it out thinly and cut nine 10 cm (4 inch) rounds. Line a 9 hole muffin tin with the dough, then chill the muffin tin for about 15 minutes.

2 Put a teaspoon of lemon curd in the base of each pastry case.

3 Mix together the curd cheese, eggs and sugar in a bowl. Divide the filling between the pastry cases and sprinkle with grated nutmeg.

4 Bake the tartlets in a preheated oven for 20–25 minutes until the filling has risen and the pastry is crisp. Dust with sifted icing sugar and serve warm or cold.

Chocolate mousse tartlets

Make sure you buy the best quality unsweetened chocolate for these tartlets, because the flavour is crucial. Look for chocolate with 70 per cent cocoa solids.

PREPARATION TIME: 25 minutes, plus chilling
COOKING TIME: 20 minutes
OVEN TEMPERATURE: 200°C (400°F), Gas Mark 6
SERVES 10

250 g (8 oz) rich shortcrust pastry
175 g (6 oz) unsweetened dark chocolate, broken into squares
2–3 tablespoons water
1 tablespoon unsalted butter, diced
1 tablespoon brandy or Cointreau
3 eggs, separated
chocolate shavings, to decorate

1 Make the pastry (*see page* 15). Roll it out and line eight 10 cm (4 inch) tartlet tins with pastry. Reroll the trimmings and line 2 more tins. Chill for 15 minutes, then bake the pastry cases blind in a preheated oven for 15 minutes. Remove the paper and beans or foil and bake for a further 5 minutes. Leave to cool.

2 Make the filling. Put the chocolate in a heatproof bowl. Add the water. Set the bowl over a pan of hot water and leave until the chocolate has melted, stirring occasionally.

3 Remove the bowl from over the water and stir in the butter until it has melted. Add the brandy or Cointreau. Stir in the egg yolks. Beat the egg whites in a clean bowl until they are stiff and dry and fold them into the chocolate mixture.

4 Spoon the mousse mixture into the tartlet cases, then transfer them to the refrigerator for 2–3 hours until set. Sprinkle with the chocolate shavings and serve cold.

Chocolate mousse tartlets

Index

Acknowledgements

PHOTOGRAPHY: © **Octopus Publishing Group Ltd**/Stephen Conroy
FOOD STYLING & ADDITIONAL RECIPES: David Morgan

EXECUTIVE EDITOR: Sarah Ford
SENIOR EDITOR: Rachel Lawrence
EXECUTIVE ART EDITOR & DESIGN: Geoff Fennell
PRODUCTION CONTROLLER: Ian Paton